Data Mining

Index of place names

Aquae Sulis – Bath
Camulodunum – Colchester
Cent - Kent
Curia – Traprain Law, East Lothian
Deva – Chester
Durobrivae - Rochester
Eburucum - York
Glevum – Gloucester
Guoloph – Nether Wallop, Hampshire
Hibernia - Ireland
Isca Dumnoniorum – Exeter
Isle of Tanatos – Isle of Thanet, Kent
Lindum - Lincoln
Londinium – Londinium
Metaris Aestuarium – The Wash, East Anglia
Mons Ambrius – Amesbury
Ratae – Leicester
Tamesas – The Thames
Venedotia – Gwynedd
Venta Icenorum – Caistor St Edmund
Vercovicium – Housesteads, Northumberland
Verulamium – Saint Albans
Viroconium - Wroxeter

"That they (The Britons) might not be brought to utter destruction, took arms under the conduct of Ambrosius Aurelianus, a modest man, who of all the Roman nation was then alone in the confusion of this troubled period by chance left alive..."

Gildas, De Excidio et Conquestu Britanniae (On the Ruin and Conquest of Britannia

AMBROSIUS

1.

It was a steel-grey morning, cold winds howling like the ghosts of slain warriors as they billowed in from the North Sea and scoured the dreary fenlands. There was no comfort to be found on that bleak stretch of coast, nothing to hide a man's shrinking skin from the lash of autumn storms.

To most of the fifty horsemen, struggling across a headland in the teeth of a gale, the blasted landscape was a glimpse of Hell. Wrapped in their thick woollen cloaks, they rode with heads bowed, dreaming of hot food, spiced wine, warm beds and pliant women.

Their leader was different. He rode with a straight back, head tilted upwards, glorying in the rawness of the cold as it cut through his layers of mail and wool and made his blood pump faster. The wind, the cry of the gulls, the pounding of the grey seas against splintered cliffs, all combined to induce a kind of euphoria in him.

His youth helped. Ambrosius Aurelianus was just seventeen years old, and riding out on his first command. His father, the Consul Aurelius, had despatched him to inspect the nine main fortresses guarding the Saxon Shore.

"Begin in the south," his father had ordered back in Londinium, placing his thick index finger against Portus Adurni, the southernmost of the chain of forts, on a map of eastern Britannia, "and work your way around the coast to Branodunum."

Ambrosius nodded impatiently. There was no need to explain the route. He knew the layout of his father's province intimately, having studied and explored most of it from an early age, as soon as he was old enough to back a horse.

Still, Aurelius was all grave formality. In the presence of his subordinates, there was no father-son relationship. Ambrosius was just another junior officer, being entrusted with a routine but important task.

"What are you to look for?" asked Aurelius, raising a thick eyebrow at his son. The Consul was a heavy man, stocky and bow-legged from a career spent mostly in the saddle, galloping from one trouble spot to another. Barely forty, he had the look of a man ten years older, all the hair rubbed from his scalp, his blunt features scored with deep lines and wrinkles.

He had good cause to look tired. Originally a civilian title, Aurelius' duties as Consul had come to embrace the upkeep of the Saxon Shore forts. This was once the responsibility of the Roman military, but since the departure of the legions it had fallen to powerful landowners like Aurelius to oversee the defence of the island.

Ambrosius cleared his throat. He knew his father's temper, and how it could suddenly explode, turning the ponderous man standing before him into a raging, purple-faced monster. It didn't happen often, but slackness and neglect of duty were two certain ways of waking the beast inside Aurelius.

"The state of the fortifications," he answered promptly, "any sign of deterioration in the walls are to be noted and reported to you. The number of men in each fort. The state of their equipment, morale and supplies. Any recent desertions, punishments and casualties."

Aurelius held his gaze for a long moment. "Good," he said finally, just as perspiration was starting to bead on Ambrosius' forehead, "I will give you fifty men. Light horse. Not enough to impress the foederati, perhaps, but I cannot spare any more."

He failed to explain why, and Ambrosius knew better than to ask. Aurelius had plenty of enemies, especially in Londinium, and preferred to keep as many armed men about him as possible.

That was over a fortnight ago. Ambrosius had proudly ridden out of Londinium at the head of his command, and headed south-west to inspect Portus Adurni.

He was now on the last stretch of his journey, between the forts of Gariannonum and Branodunum. These lay on the eastern seaboard of his father's province of Maxima Caesariensis, the largest of the five Roman provinces of Britannia. It was also the only one still properly administered as such. Cut loose from

Roman rule, the rest of the country was slowly reverting to a patchwork of tribal territories.

Ambrosius' mood clouded a little. All had not gone as smoothly as he, or his father, would have liked. True, the garrisons of the forts had received him with the respect due to a son of the Consul, but what he had seen was not encouraging.

The forts were garrisoned by foederati, descendents of Germanic sea-pirates given land on the eastern coasts of Britannia by former Roman governors, and encouraged to settle. Their sons and grandsons, it was reasoned, would defend the land they now occupied. Thus Rome made use of barbarians to fight barbarians.

It was a policy employed all over the Western Empire to make up for the desperate lack of manpower. To Ambrosius, born in Londinium but raised to think of himself as Roman, the policy on the Saxon Shore was both humiliating and short-sighted.

Barbarians are barbarians, he thought to himself as he gazed out to sea, *and will naturally side with their own kin, no matter how much land and gold we bribe them with.*

The fort of Rutupiae had caused him particular concern. Once garrisoned by a thousand legionaries of the II Augusta, it was now held by less than a hundred foederati troops. Discipline at the fort was slack. The sentry that saluted him at the gate was clearly drunk, and struggled to remain upright as he saluted.

Old-fashioned virtues of Roman martial discipline and order had been drummed into Ambrosius from childhood.

"Your man at the gate is the worse for drink," he snapped after exchanging formal greetings with the commander of the fort, "assemble your men in the yard and give him twenty-five lashes. Now."

The commander, a tall, pop-eyed Jute with wine stains down the front of his tunic, hastened to apologise. "You must excuse the man, sir," he pleaded, "today is my birthday, and I allowed the men to drink my health. The fault is mine."

"Perhaps I should flog you instead," Ambrosius replied drily, and was secretly amused to see the blood drain from the man's face, "but that would be bad for discipline."

The punishment was duly carried out, and the garrison troops looked on in sullen silence as their comrade was given a bloody back by the drill-master.

While the guilty party howled under the lash, Ambrosius looked over the soldiers. Third or fourth-generation barbarians, a rabble of Jutes, Saxons and Frisians from the northern wastes of Germania. Their forefathers had come to Britannia to ravage and plunder, and ended up staying to defend it.

The flogging at Rutupiae proved a one-off. Ambrosius encountered no further breaches of discipline at the remaining forts, or at least none that warranted his intervention. The foederati were second-rate troops at best, and couldn't be expected to do much more than guard their bit of coastline.

Sometimes, even that limited duty proved beyond them. Ambrosius and his men were a few miles from Branadunum when one of his officers appeared at his elbow.

"Smoke to the north-west, sir," he murmured, pointing his javelin in that direction.

Ambrosius' head snapped around. At first he saw nothing, no tell-tale wisps of smoke rising from the endless marshy flatlands.

"You have good eyes, decurio," he said, "better than mine, even though they are twenty years younger."

The decurio, whose name was Menas, smiled briefly. A tough veteran, originally hailing from the Wall, Aurelius had despatched him to serve his son as second-in-command. In reality he was there to look after him, and make sure the young man did nothing foolish.

Ambrosius realised this, but appreciated Menas' presence. The veteran was a great comfort, and he made few decisions without consulting him first.

Then he saw it. A faint trail of blackish smoke, drifting lazily over the horizon to the north-west.

"About three miles inland, sir," said Menas.

Ambrosius thought rapidly. Branodunum was some five miles away, roughly in the same direction. If there had been a raid, the garrison should have sallied out to deal with it.

A careful band of pirates might have crept inland undetected, in which case the fort commander was guilty of dereliction. He should have had scouts posted all along the coast, tasked with lighting beacons on the cliff-tops when raiders were sighted.

He quickly scanned the sea. No sign of any ships. Apart from the threat of Germanic pirates, Pictish raiding parties were becoming increasingly common in this region. They sailed their longboats down from the north, bypassing the Wall, and penetrated inland, following the waterways around Lindum and Metaris Aestuarium.

Ambrosius forced himself to be calm. Perhaps the fire was nothing. An accident, perhaps, or some farmer burning his rubbish.

He was about to ask Menas for advice, but stopped. It was time he learned to make his own decisions. Born into a noble Roman family, his lot in life was to provide leadership, whether in the council chamber or the battlefield.

"We should take a closer look," he said, and led his men inland at a canter, trying to follow a direct line towards the smoke.

It was many years since Ambrosius had explored this remote part of the province, and none of his men were natives. But for the good sense of Menas, they might have blundered into a miles-wide stretch of impassable bog, and spent hours struggling out of it.

"I advise you to turn back, sir, and follow the coast," he said quietly when they reached the edge of the fen, "if there are pirates hereabouts, they might have rowed their boats up an inlet. Perhaps we can find the mouth of the river and follow it inland."

Ambrosius stared glumly at the wall of reeds before him, hiding a world of unseen dangers, and at the smoke rising into the sky a couple of miles beyond. He would have preferred to ride straight on, but it was impossible. There were no roads here, and such pathways as existed were well-hidden.

"We need a guide," he said, slapping away the flies trying to crawl inside his helmet, "some native bog-dweller, who can show us a safe path through this morass."

Menas shrugged his heavy shoulders. "There are none, sir. All in hiding, I'll wager."

Lacking any other option, Ambrosius consented to Menas' plan, and led his men back to the shore.

They worked their way along the rugged line of the cliffs, occasionally descending to sandy beaches, while the wind continued to howl and tear at the exposed coastline. The thunder of churning seas echoed inside Ambrosius' head, filling him with renewed vigour.

More smoke soon became visible, rising from the direction of Branodunum. The fort itself remained out of sight, hidden behind some rising ground.

Ambrosius feared some disaster had befallen the fort, which was the most isolated of all those guarding the Saxon Shore. Fearful images passed through his mind of a huge band of sea-pirates, hundreds strong, descending on the unwary garrison and butchering the lot of them, before penetrating inland to sack the neighbouring villages.

Ambrosius started to feel foolish. The smoke was probably rising from the fort's kitchens and cooking fires. He was nervous, on edge, snatching at every doom-laden explanation.

At last, barely a mile from the fort, they found a little sandy bay enclosed on the landward side by a range of black cliffs.

There was no inlet leading inland from the bay, but a narrow path was worn into the eastern flank of the cliffs. Drawn up on the pale yellow sand was a type of longboat. It had a single mast, the sail furled, and tapered at both ends to a narrow prow and stern.

Ambrosius stared down at it from the cliff-edge overlooking the bay. The boat was of a type the Saxons called a keel, and large enough to carry over twenty warriors.

Just one, though. For all he knew, there might be more keels resting inside secluded bays up and down the coast.

That was muddled thinking. Ambrosius willed himself to be decisive. There was no use dithering over uncertainties.

He twisted his head to look at the puffs of smoke. In his mind's eye he saw the light of burning cottages, and thought he heard the distant screams of defenceless crofters and fishermen being slaughtered by blood-crazed barbarians.

His eye followed the line of the path from the cliff. It quickly vanished into a maze of reed-beds and shallow waterways, but the land immediately to the west looked slightly firmer.

"Come," he said, clapping in his spurs, "I smell pirates."

2.

The horsemen picked their way through a desolate landscape of undulating sand banks, narrow rivulets and patches of scrubby woodland. All was silence, save for the moaning of the ever-present wind and the jingle of harness.

The sun was high in the sky now, and a flash of light caught Ambrosius' eye.

He signalled at his men to halt and leaned forward in the saddle, straining to make out the source of the light.

There it was again. Sunlight, glinting on metal.

"Well?" he asked Menas, "what do you make of it, hawk-eyes?"

The veteran shaded his eyes and gazed east. "Spears," he murmured, "I count a dozen, maybe more. They are coming this way. Men on foot."

Ambrosius' heart beat faster. This was what he had been trained for. All the thousands of hours of drill and weapons exercise were about to culminate in this moment. His first real fight.

He gulped down his excitement. As the officer in charge, he had to keep a clear head.

"Order the men to spread out, either side of the standard," he said, striving to keep his voice steady, "we will advance at a trot, in loose skirmish order, and close on my signal."

His standard bearer, a young man named Licinius, held aloft a long pole topped with a dragon's head forged of iron, its toothy maw gaping open to the wind.

Attached to its neck was a long sleeve made of pieces of cloth, dyed red and sewn together. As Licinius spurred forward, the wind passed through the tube, making it ripple like a serpent and emit a whistling noise. This draco or dragon standard had been adopted from the tribes of Scythia by the cavalry units of the Roman legions, who in turn passed in to the Britons.

Menas' harsh voice barked out the order to advance. Ambrosius puffed out his cheeks, smiled at the pale-faced

Licinius with a confidence he didn't feel, and gently goaded his horse into a trot.

The wind lashed the dragon into life as they advanced. Ambrosius fancied the beast had come alive, its iron jaws ready to snap shut, long serpentine tail fluttering in anticipation of a kill.

I must be the dragon, he thought, *savage and merciless.*

His hands were sweating. The oval shield strapped to his left arm felt strangely heavy, and the shaft of the throwing javelin in his right hand kept slipping.

Steady, you fool! Your men look to you for leadership. Do not shame your father!

His father. The mere thought of Aurelius, fleshy features swelling with rage as he heard of his son's embarrassing performance, stiffened Ambrosius' wilting courage. Better dead, spitted on a Saxon blade, than risk the old man's wrath.

The spear-heads were clearly visible now, glinting over the rise of a sand dune less than forty yards to the west. Their owners jogged into view.

Saxons.

His eye swiftly took them in. Eighteen men. Tall, muscular warriors armed with shields and spears. No body armour, save their chief, who wore a helmet with dangling cheek-pieces and a ring-mail byrnie reaching to his knees.

The chief and his leading men stopped dead on the crest of the dune. Judging from their hesitation, they hadn't expected to meet any opposition.

Behind them, now less than a quarter of a mile away, the wisp of black smoke Menas had first spotted from the coast rose into the sky. The Saxons must have landed, under cover of darkness, and darted inland to put some settlement to the torch.

Ambrosius' fears were confirmed when he saw five of the warriors dragging prisoners behind them on lengths of rope. Three women and two young children, their wrists tightly bound together, grubby peasant faces raw with burns and tears.

The sight of these helpless souls, doomed to be carried off to live and die as slaves in some stinking barbarian village, filled Ambrosius with cold rage. His fears dissolved like morning mist.

He flung up his right arm. "Charge!" he shouted, and drove in his spurs.

Licinius blew the signal to attack on his bugle, but the horsemen were already flowing over the dunes.

Ambrosius galloped straight towards the Saxon chief, who was bellowing orders in his strange, guttural tongue. To Ambrosius, it sounded like the grunting of a frightened pig.

Outnumbered and surprised, most of the Saxons panicked. The chief managed to rally four and hustle them into a line on the crest, shields overlapping. Two carried angons, short throwing spears almost entirely made of iron, and drew them back, ready to cast.

The rest scattered, fleeing back the way they had come or scrambling on their backsides down the steep flanks of the dune.

Ambrosius saw one of the prisoners fling herself at her captor, trying to snatch his saex from the leather scabbard hanging from his belt. He seized a handful of her greasy hair and flung her to one side, cursing as she left bite-marks on his wrist.

Instinct, and long years of military training, took over. Ambrosius wheeled his horse sharply to the left as she reached the base of the dune, and in the same movement hurled his javelin at the Saxon chief.

It was a good throw, but the other man was quick, and caught the javelin on his shield. The iron tip struck the ox-hide covering, but failed to penetrate the wood beneath.

Ambrosius' men cast their javelins. Three of the Saxons on the crest went down, their bodies fatally pierced. Screams and oaths cut through the air as their fleeing comrades were hunted through the dunes, speared and hacked down without mercy.

The chief seemed unconcerned. He bellowed in fierce war-delight and clashed his sword against his mailed chest as the British cavalry surged up the slope.

Ambrosius tore out his spatha, a long cavalry sword with a heavy chopping edge, and charged straight at him.

AMBROSIUS

His opponent was big, far bigger than he first thought. The muscles of the Saxon's brawny shoulders and upper arms bunched as he got well behind his shield. Ambrosius' javelin was still stuck fast in the covering, but he was strong enough to prevent the extra weight dragging his shield down.

The other warrior was swiftly butchered, cut to pieces from three sides at once. He stood by his master to the last, chanting oaths until a spatha chopped into his throat.

Ambrosius cut down with all his strength at the chief's shield. The Saxon stood like a rock under the blow, and responded with a sly thrust of his sword. His bright blade flickered like a serpent's tongue as it stabbed at the belly of Ambrosius' horse.

"Pig," Ambrosius spat, knocking aside the thrust in time. He had to lean downward slightly, exposing his head to the boss of the Saxon's shield.

He knew how Saxons fought, their aggressive use of shields in combat, but it was one thing to know, another to counter.

The thick iron boss smashed into Ambrosius' face. His nose crunched, pain flooded through his jaw, and the warm salt tang of blood filled his mouth. He was stunned, defenceless. The Saxon's sword stabbed again, this time at his heart.

Fortunately, he also wore mail, a fine steel coat his late mother had presented to him shortly before her death the previous year. The links were small, much smaller than Saxon ring-mail, and the tip of the blade scraped harmlessly against his metal skin.

Pain and terror brought Ambrosius to his senses. His bleeding face was mere inches from his opponent's, so close he could see the green irises through the eye-holes of the other man's helm, and smell the taint of mead and fish on his breath.

Ambrosius struck upwards. The hilt of his spatha punched the Saxon in the mouth, forcing him to stagger back a few steps, far enough for Ambrosius to try another cut at him.

The edge of his spatha sheared into the Saxon's neck, half-decapitating him and spilling a gush of blood down the front of his byrnie, dyeing the yellow sand a visceral shade of red.

It was a fine blow, of the sort Ambrosius had practised many times, usually on helmets or cabbages stuck on the end of poles.

He had never fought in earnest before, never spilled blood except by accident while sparring. Never really tried to kill a man.

Now it was done, and the Saxon chief was on his knees, gasping his life out.

For one absurd moment Ambrosius thought he should dismount and help him. His father's craggy face rose in his mind, twisted into a sneer.

"You're too soft-hearted, boy," Aurelius was fond of saying, "just like your mother, God rest her. The Lord has seen fit to give me a girl in man's clothing for a son. If I had more sons, you would be for the church. I have none, so you must learn how to play the man."

Aurelius wanted a son forged in his own image: hard, ruthless, practical. Ambrosius strove to live up to his father's standards, but he was by nature gentle and merciful, and sometimes found himself behaving with unnecessary cruelty to make up for it.

There was nothing gentle about the Saxon's death. He gasped and shuddered out his last, a red tide pouring from the unsightly gash in his throat, and flopped forward onto the sand, fingers scrabbling for purchase.

Ambrosius watched the man die with a mixture of horror and fascination. The triumphant shouts of his men echoed around the desolate landscape as they hunted down the remaining Saxons.

His victim's body gave a final spasm and went still. Only then did Ambrosius raise a hand to his face to probe the ruin of his nose. His lower lip was bruised and swollen, and he spat out a gobbet of blood.

Menas cantered up the slope. "Well done, sir," he said cheerfully, "your first kill, and your first victory. Shame we didn't get to the village in time to save it, but that wasn't your fault. Those sluggards at Branodunum have a lot of explaining to do."

Ambrosius forgot his own trifling woes and glanced west. From the summit of the dune, he could see a little group of huts, pathetic little timber roundhouses with conical thatched roofs, gathered inside a rough stockade of stakes.

AMBROSIUS

Most of the huts had been burned. Some of the inhabitants lay strewn about outside, their bodies hacked to pieces, like so many joints of beef. The stockade, a flimsy protection at the best of times, had offered none against the fury of the sea-wolves.

Ambrosius imagined the Saxons descending on the place at night, smashing down the gate or swarming over the stakes, before setting about their grim work.

A wave of reaction swept over him. He felt sick, and started to tremble, as though seized by a sudden fever.

"Steady," said Menas, placing a heavy hand on his shoulder, "best not to heave your guts up in front of the men, eh? Don't fret. This happens to all of us. I remember my first kill. A Pict, he was, a scrawny, bare-arsed savage with a long red beard and tattoos all over him. I had to go behind a bush, where the decurio couldn't see me, and lose my breakfast."

Ambrosius gritted his teeth and tried to compose himself. Menas was right. He could not show weakness in front of the men.

He staved off the nausea by concentrating on Branadunum. If the garrison had done their duty, none of this slaughter and bloodshed would have come to pass. The villagers would still be alive, and he would not be faced with the task of comforting the few survivors.

When he had mastered himself again, Ambrosius ordered Licinius to sound the recall. His men rode back – all of them, thank God – some carrying the severed heads of dead Saxons tied by the hair to their saddles.

Ambrosius was appalled. "We are Christian soldiers, not barbarians!" he shouted, "get rid of those damned things at once."

With some reluctance, his men obeyed, and threw away their grisly trophies. Ambrosius ordered them to look for the prisoners, who had scattered when their Saxon captors tried to flee.

They found none, save the body of one of the children. A little girl, no more than six or seven years old. Her throat had been slashed, probably by the Saxon who took her captive.

The fresh tides of nausea and anger that swept through Ambrosius as he looked down at the tiny, blood-spattered body were almost too much to bear. His head swam, and he swayed dangerously in the saddle, like a fragile tree buffeted by storms.

"To Branadunum," he said thickly, and turned his horse's head towards the fort.

3.

Vortigern disliked Londinium, and visited as rarely as possible. The old capital of the Roman province of Britannia was a symbol of all the things he despised and sought to undermine: the lingering authority of the Roman state, the power of the orthodox Christian church and (not least) the power of Aurelius. Vortigern was too proud to admit to fearing any man, but he harboured a secret dread of the Consul, his chief rival.

Since the departure of the legions, true power in Britannia lay with those who commanded the most warriors. The mathematics of it was brutally simple. Vortigern had five hundred buccelari, mounted cavalry, which made him the most important man in the country. Aurelius could muster three hundred, making him the second.

"Curse the man," Vortigern muttered. His voice died away in the vast, echoing stillness of the hall.

This was the meeting-place of the Council Of Britannia. It was a huge rotunda of marble and white stone in the centre of the vast complex of the governor's palace. Here the Vicarius, the Roman governor of Britannia, used to meet with his advisors.

The rotunda was a typically splendid Roman building, with colonnaded walls and a mosaic on the floor, the tessarae of which displayed beautifully realised images of hunting scenes, pagan gods, naked lovers strolling or copulating among the greenwood, marching legions and long-dead Emperors.

There was no Vicarius anymore. The last one had left with the legions, leaving the Britons to elect a High King in his place. As the man with the largest number of soldiers under his command, Vortigern had secured the crown with little difficulty.

He sat at a round table, a hollow wooden circle, big enough to seat the twenty-five members of the council. The round table was his idea, a way of making all the councillors feel like equals.

Not too equal, of course. Vortigern had the biggest chair, and the mailed and helmed guards on the door served as an eloquent reminder of where power truly lay in Britannia.

He braced himself as voices and footsteps echoed down the corridor outside the rotunda.

Aurelius swaggered into the room, deep in conversation with Flavius Sanctus and Lucius Septimius, governors of Venta Icenorum and Camulodunum respectively. Both towns lay inside the Consul's province, and the governors were close friends and allies of his.

Vortigern gripped the arms of his chair. If they showed him the faintest hint of disrespect...

All three ceased talking and bowed in his direction before taking their seats. He relaxed slightly.

An uncomfortable silence fell. Save in formal council, Vortigern had nothing to say to neither these men, nor they to him. They could hardly resume their conversation in the presence of the High King, and so all four sat like mutes, carefully avoiding each other's eyes.

Well might they remain silent, Vortigern thought bitterly, *and keep their lying tongues behind the fence of their teeth.*

They resent me, think I am nothing, a jumped-up native princeling, seeking to overthrow their precious Roman traditions. You may as well choke on your resentment, traitors. I will be in power long after you are quiet in your graves.

The rest of the councillors filed in, a motley collection of rich landowners, official representatives of various towns and cities, and tribal kings.

These last came robed and dripping with finery. They wore plain bands of gold or silver on their brows, and carried swords with richly decorated hilts. More gold gleamed at their wrists and throats, and their cloaks were lined with rabbit fur or soft lamb's wool.

Vortigern approved of all this display. Britannia was a land of tribes, or had been before the legions arrived and subjugated them.

Now the Romans were gone, he wanted to restore the old customs. That was his dream. Before his time was done, he would make it a reality, using whatever means came to hand.

Whatever means...

AMBROSIUS

Vortigern slowly rose to his feet. The councillors did likewise, and the hall briefly echoed to the scrape of chairs being pushed back, the rustle of wool and furs and the clank of weapons.

"Welcome to you all," he said gruffly, "the council will now begin."

As opening speeches went, it lacked grandeur. Vortigern liked to think of himself as a plain, uncomplicated man of his hands, and had no skill with words.

Twenty-four faces stared back at him. Most were carefully blank, but Vortigern thought he detected a flicker of amusement or even contempt on a few.

Aurelius' hard grey eyes were gazing at him without a trace of fear. Or respect.

Vortigern decided to strike his blow. He had planned to save it until the very end of the council, when more pressing issues had been discussed, but the Consul's presence was already wearing on his nerves.

"First, let us deal with an unpleasant matter," he said, settling back into his chair, "namely your son, Aurelius."

He was gratified to see the other man's face pale a little. There was something invincible about Aurelius. A large, powerfully-built man, he was not easily shaken.

"What of him?" the Consul demanded, laying his big hands flat on the table. His friends, Flavius and Lucius, glanced nervously at him.

"You know very well," Vortigern went on, "some three weeks past, he slew a Saxon chief named Wiglaf."

"Wiglaf was a pirate," Aurelius snapped, "he and his vermin had attacked and destroyed a village near Branadunum. Ambrosius was merely doing his duty, unlike the local garrison."

Vortigern laced his hands together. Warm afternoon sunlight slanted through the latticed windows and flashed off the rings adorning his fingers. They were made of dark red gold, mined in the far west of Britannia. The one on the middle finger of his right hand was studded with a large, square-cut piece of amethyst. It was one of his most treasured possessions, found inside a chest of jewellery left behind by the last Vicarius.

The High King was started to enjoy himself. "Ah yes, the garrison. After killing this alleged pirate and his men, Ambrosius further distinguished himself by riding to the fort and summarily executing its commander."

He slowly leaned forward. "Executed without trial," he said, looking around meaningfully at the councillors, "hanged from the walls of his own fort."

Aurelius' hands bunched into fists. "Military justice," he growled, "the man wasn't fit to live. Clear dereliction of duty. His job was to protect that stretch of coast. He failed, and gave no adequate reasons for his failure. Claimed he didn't even see the Saxons landing. Didn't see them! They torch a village barely two miles from his post, and he has the gall to say that. There were no sentries or watch-fires placed along the cliffs either."

Vortigern let him speak. The Consul was lumbering straight into an ambush.

"The commander of Branadunum was a Jute," Aurelius added, "for all we know, he was in league with the pirates, or Wiglaf might have thrown him a handful of gold to do nothing while the villagers were robbed and murdered."

A murmur ran around the table.

Vortigern held up his hand for silence. "Enough, Aurelius," he said, allowing a hint of severity to creep into his voice, "it is hardly fitting to speak so ill of the dead, who cannot speak for themselves. Ambrosius acted hastily and without judgment. He is very young. Too young, perhaps, to be entrusted with overseeing the Saxon Shore."

"As for the commander being a Jute," he continued before Aurelius could respond, "it has long been our policy to garrison the forts with Saxon warriors and their kin."

"A policy I have always disagreed with," Aurelius said hotly, "those forts should be stuffed full of British soldiers, not Germanic sea-filth. How can we trust them to defend our shores against their own people? This latest incident is but further proof that the policy must change. Grant me permission, lord king, to levy soldiers from the towns inside my province, and use them to re-garrison the forts of the Saxon Shore."

This met with some approval. Lucius went so far as to clap.

"That would mean war, Aurelius," Vortigern replied smoothly, "the foederati have occupied those forts for decades now. They were born and raised on British soil. Their families live outside the walls. If you try and remove them, they will fight."

He might have said, *and I have no intention of granting you permission to raise a private army.* Aurelius' three hundred buccelari made him dangerous enough already. The population of the towns inside his province had dwindled away in recent years, but there were still enough able-bodied men to provide him with not less than a thousand auxiliaries.

Vortigern regarded Aurelius as a relic, a throwback to the high days of the Western Empire. The council had permitted him to take the title of Consul, a term that had almost fallen into disuse, and lord it over the old Roman province of Maxima Caesaeriensis. Since he was the wealthiest landowner in the region, he could hardly be denied without risking a war.

The fool wanted Britannia to return to the imperial fold. He wanted the legions back again. Vortigern preferred to deal in reality. The Empire was split in two, and the western half bleeding its life out from a multitude of wounds, many of them self-inflicted.

No, the days of the Western Empire were done. New powers were rising, vigorous young barbarian races from the east, principally Germania. Vortigern intended to make Britannia part of this new world, not a useless appendage of the old.

"Returning to Ambrosius," he said, "I am willing to disregard the execution of the fort's commander. Possibly there were good reasons for it. But the blood-price must be paid for the death of Wiglaf, pirate or no."

"If you imagine I am going to hand over my son to the Saxons for punishment..." Aurelius began angrily, but Vortigern waved him into silence.

"Don't be a fool. You know the customs of these folk. They want compensation for the loss of their kinsman. Wiglaf was the son of a gesith, and his blood-price is set at four hundred head of cattle. Half the cattle and thirty slaves would also be acceptable."

Aurelius shot to his feet. "Who is making these demands?" he roared, "since when did we allow these accursed barbarians to dictate to us?"

"Resume your seat," Vortigern shouted back, raising his voice for the first time, "even now, two hundred Saxon warriors are encamped on the southern shore of the Tamesas, awaiting our reply. I had the demand from their chief, Guechta."

The Consul remained standing. "Lord king," he said in a more level voice, though his face was white and blotchy with barely-suppressed rage, "permit me to ride out with my household guards and clear away these vermin. Let them learn what it means to threaten the Council of Britannia. By nightfall, I shall bring you the head of their chief."

Vortigern smirked. "I am not about to let you compound your son's mistakes. Hundreds more of Wiglaf's kinsmen are poised across the sea, waiting for the signal to descend upon our shores like a pack of starving wolves. Your province would be the first to suffer their wrath. I daresay you would be glad of the foederati then."

A tight thrill of pleasure ran through him. He had won. Aurelius enjoyed no support from his fellow councillors – even Flavius and Lucius were silent – and after a long moment he sank back into his seat, humiliated.

"Livestock and slaves," the High King said firmly, "to be delivered ten days from now. You are a rich man, and can afford it. If we refuse to pay, Guechta will sail his keels upriver and lay waste to our farms and villas. The blood-price is also the price of peace."

Vortigern failed to add that he had already come to a private understanding with Guechta. Once the money was paid, the Saxon chief and his warriors would enter Vortigern's service as foederati, and be given land on the south-east coast of Britannia.

It was a bold strategy, with severe risks. The High King enjoyed the support of roughly half the council, but was suspicious of the remainder. There were too many Romans among them, wealthy landowners who had elected to stay in

Britannia after the legions left. Aurelius was the most prominent, but there were others.

If these men knew Vortigern intended to invite more and more Saxon warriors to Britannia, they would be horrified. To them, the Saxons were mere barbarians, to be employed as garrison troops only when strictly necessary. Enticing them over in large numbers, to be given good British farmland and encouraged to settle, would be perceived as rank treachery.

Vortigern couldn't ignore the Romans, but he meant to push them aside. Consign them to irrelevance. He already commanded the largest war-band in Britannia. With an army of Saxon mercenaries at his disposal, he could reign supreme.

He eyed Aurelius with particular loathing. The Consul would not live much longer, Vortigern decided, and nor would his troublesome son.

4.

A storm whipped through the narrow band of sea lying between the coast of Gaul and Britannia, churning the waters into a hellish maelstrom, unfit for any vessel to sail.

Any vessel, save one commissioned on the Lord's work.

Truly, thought Germanus, Bishop of Auxerre, *there is a storm in Heaven. Is the realm of the Lord divided, as we are on earth?*

His long, thin arms were wrapped tightly around the mainmast, and he ignored the screams of the crew ordering him to get below.

Germanus realised he was in their way, but God was testing him. This was merely the first of the trials he would face on his divine mission. Fail now, run away from the wrath of the storm, and his conviction would die inside him.

Germanus thrived on conviction. The holy spirit filled him like a raging, unquenchable fire, driving him on to push his mortal form to breaking point.

For all that, he was frightened. The sea frightened him, the storm-black skies, the crack of thunder and stab-stab-stab of lightning. He had never been to sea before, and had accepted the risk of attempting the crossing in the depths of winter with a blithe assurance that now seemed insane.

A foaming green wave rose before him and smashed against the prow of the ship, almost throwing her onto her beam-ends.

"God preserve us," Germanus shouted. His words were swallowed up by the storm, and his grip on the mast shaken loose. For a second his sandaled feet scrabbled for purchase on a deck tilted at a terrifying angle, and then he fell backwards, limbs flailing as he flew through the air.

He landed with a bone-jarring crash against the rail. The ship had righted herself, else he would have been swept over the side, and he was able to snatch at a trailing bit of rope.

Strong hands closed on his bony forearm and hauled him to his feet. The captain of the ship, a hairy, black-gummed Gaul named Samo, grabbed a fistful of Germanus' tunic.

"Listen, Your Grace," he snarled, thrusting his dripping face close to the bishop's, "you will get below right now, or I'll drag you down the ladder myself. Understand?"

Samo was a typically burly sailor, built along the same lines as an ape, with long, powerful arms and muscular shoulders from a life spent crawling up and down the rigging. By contrast, Germanus was a weak and feeble man, his strength drained by regular fasting and a deliberately poor diet. Since he took the tonsure – or rather, had it forced on him – he had eaten nothing but coarse barley bread once a day, the grains threshed and ground with his own hands.

The Gaul could have snapped him in half without too much effort, but Germanus had no fear of men.

"Do not presume to threaten me," he cried, "I am a servant of the Lord, and your immortal soul trembles on the edge of the abyss. I have it in my power to haul you back from the brink, or damn you for all time."

His voice rose above the swirling chaos of the storm like a trumpet. Samo's brutish face turned a sickly shade of grey, and he released his grip on Germanus' tunic as though it had suddenly burst into flames.

The captain's fear gave Germanus renewed confidence. This storm was nothing, a mere illusion sent by the Devil to shake his resolve.

Satan would have to work a good deal harder. Germanus' companion, Lupus, the Bishop of Troyes, had been driven below by sea-sickness, but it would take more than a bit of noise and a few puffs of wind to crack the iron will of the Bishop of Auxerre.

He raised his hand to the little box hanging from a chain around his neck. The box contained a collection of holy relics: saint's bones, mostly, and a small flask of blessed oil. Germanus always carried it on his person, relying on the undoubted power of the relics to bring him good fortune.

An idea struck him. Perhaps the oil could soothe the raging waters of the tempest.

Bellowing prayers, Germanus clung to the rail with one hand and carefully snapped open the lid of the box with the other. The random lurching of the ship in tormented seas, the wild heaving of the deck under his feet, was nothing to him now. He was a rock, and would not be shifted by any power on earth.

He took out the flask, ripped out the stopper with his teeth, and upended it over the side. A thin trickle of oil flowed out of the flask and splashed into the raging waves below.

"You need have no fear, captain," Germanus shouted confidently, stuffing the empty flask back into its box, "the holy blessed oil shall render these seas smooth as glass. We are in God's hands, and God wants us to reach the Island of Britannia unharmed."

Samo said nothing, though Germanus read the doubt on his face. He could have laughed. When would men learn to trust in the might of the Lord?

The storm did die down, though not as swiftly as Germanus would have liked. For another two hours the ship, a bulky three-mast merchant vessel, was tortured by the elements. She rode at anchor, and the crew could do little but plug any leaks and join the two holy men in their prayers.

Then it was over. The storm fled, as suddenly as it had come, leaving a pale, washed-out sky and calm grey seas. Germanus exulted in his triumph – or rather, God's triumph – and climbed down the ladder to inform Lupus of the miracle.

"You blessed the oil yourself, at Troyes," he said to the pale, emaciated figure lying trembling under a pile of blankets and sailcloth, "be comforted, my friend. Your illness will soon pass."

Both men were in their mid-forties, and prematurely aged by lives of merciless self-denial. Lupus, however, was of a slightly more practical turn of mind than his companion, and less prone to high-flown rhetoric.

"I wish it would pass a little sooner," he groaned, clutching his belly, "my guts are on fire. It may be a sin to pray for death, but there were times during the storm when I contemplated it."

Germanus smiled. For some reason the sea-sickness had passed him by, though he would have gladly embraced it. The mortification of the flesh was essential. Only through pain could one's soul be cleansed and purified.

AMBROSIUS

The bishop wore a hair shirt under his filthy tunic. His skin itched continuously, and crawled with lice, but the discomfort was scarcely adequate. It was only proper for him to share in Lupus' torment. Perhaps, if he had the time later, he could flog himself a little. The scars on his back from the last flogging had barely healed, and there was a good chance they would crack open and bleed afresh.

"Leave me be, I beg you," Lupus pleaded, tugging a blanket over his raddled face, "I must fight this battle alone."

After a final blessing, Germanus left him alone with his misery and returned to deck.

"Land in sight," Captain Samo informed him, "look there."

The captain pointed north, towards a distant line of white cliffs. He was still nervous of the bishop, and shuffled aside to make room for him on the foredeck.

"Britannia," breathed Germanus, shading his eyes to squint at the horizon, "the lost province. Have you visited the island before, captain?"

Samo shrugged his heavy shoulders. "Only the ports along the southern coast. It seems prosperous enough. Rains a lot. That's all I know."

He abruptly turned his broad back on Germanus, cutting off the conversation.

The bishop was content to let silence reign. Samo and his crew were simple men, secular men, ill at ease with the grandeur and sanctity of their passengers: two of the most prominent clergymen in the Western Empire, on a holy mission to the benighted island of Britannia.

Germanus gazed at the white smudge of the cliff-line, and reflected on what he knew of Britannia's recent history.

Almost twenty years past, Rome had abandoned its northernmost province, and withdrawn the last of the legions stationed there. A few Roman officials and landowners chose to remain, but otherwise the Britons were left to fend for themselves against endless waves of barbarians.

Saxon pirates ravaged the southern and eastern coasts, while the savage Scotti did the same in the west. The Wall, that increasingly fragile bastion, was repeatedly battered by the Picts. They had already broken through once, back in the days of the Emperor Valentinian, and only a mighty effort by the Roman military had driven them back again.

Britannia faced a new danger, one that (in Germanus' view) posed a far greater threat than all the barbarian peoples combined. A Pict could only slay a man's body, but now the souls of the Britons were in danger. Germanus and his companion had been tasked by the Pope to rescue them.

"Agricola."

Germanus grimaced as he rolled the hateful name around his mouth.

Agricola was a bishop, a Briton by birth. Some years previously, he had returned to his native land and started to preach the creed of Pelagianism. Named after Pelagius, the wretched ascetic who invented it, this alternative version of Christianity believed that humanity was untainted by original sin, and mortals were capable of choosing between good and evil without Divine aid.

In essence, it meant that new-born children did not have to be baptised, and the entire concept of sin was a lie.

Even now, after so many years studying the teachings of Pelagius, they had the power to make Germanus' gorge rise. He felt physically sick at the thought of Agricola and his disciples spreading their false doctrine, dripping heretical poison into the minds of the Britons – shepherding them away from the love and truth of Christ, into the arms of the Dark One!

As he always did in moments of passion, Germanus was starting to sweat. "Hoist more sail," he growled at Samo, "God's work cannot wait."

The captain ignored him. It was a foolish request anyway. All three masts were crowded with sail, and a strong south-east wind was propelling the ship lightly across the waters.

He wondered what kind of reception they would receive. The High King himself, Vortigern, was said to have succumbed to the Pelagian disease, along with many of his nobles. Perhaps he would be waiting on the shore with his soldiers, ready to greet the missionaries with cold steel.

Germanus straightened his back. If God willed it, he was ready to die a martyr's death. So, doubtless, was Lupus, assuming the sea-sickness didn't kill him first.

Slightly to the bishop's disappointment, no violent martyrdom awaited them. There were people gathered on the cliffs, and more clustered thickly on the golden beaches below, many thousands strong. The sound of their voices raised in song drifted across the water, a rapturous Te Deum mingled with other psalms.

Lupus struggled onto deck. He walked supported by a Gaulish sailor on his left arm, and a staff in his right hand.

"We should go ashore at once," he said, peering towards the shore, now less than a mile away, "lest the Britons think we are afraid."

Germanus agreed, and asked Captain Samo for a longboat. He responded with, it seemed to the bishop, slightly suspicious enthusiasm, roaring at his men to ready the boat and assemble a crew to row the holy men ashore.

"Good fortune, Your Grace," Samo remarked as Germanus and Lupus were lowered on ropes into the boat, "if that mob on the beach turns nasty, don't expect me to come and rescue you."

"The blessing of God be upon you, captain," Lupus replied sweetly in return.

The oarsmen rowed quickly to the shore, and Germanus was able to pick out individuals among the horde gathered on the beach.

"There," he said, pointing at a group of richly-dressed men in the front rank, "those are the ones we need. Do you see any who might be Vortigern?"

Lupus gripped the edge of the prow with his bony fingers, his weak eyes narrowing as he strained to see. "I know little of British customs," he murmured, "but none of those men have the look of a king. I see no royal banners, no cloth of purple and gold."

"Vortigern snubs us," Germanus said grimly, "fool. Does he think he can defy the will of Rome? His throne shall shake for this."

When the boat reached the shallows, Germanus climbed over the side and lowered himself carefully into the freezing, waist-deep waters. Lupus followed, though he was still feeble and had to be helped by the oarsmen.

"May our stay in Britannia be a long one," he said, gasping at the cold touch of the water, "that is the last time I attempt a sea-voyage in

winter."

Together, with Germanus holding his friend's arm to steady him, they waded through the surf. Many of the people waiting on the beach surged forward to meet them, cheering and singing as they splashed through the shallows, waving banners emblazoned with the sign of the cross.

Germanus lingered a while, teeth chattering, to bless over those who bowed their heads and knelt in the water before him. He was warmed a little by their enthusiasm. Evidently the curse of Pelagianism had not yet overtaken the whole country.

Numbed to the bone, he seized Lupus' wrist and pulled him towards the shore, where the British nobles waited.

Their leader was a stout, balding, tough-looking man, with the look of a soldier about him. He wore a white tunic with a purple hem under his fur-trimmed red cloak, indicating a man of senatorial or consular rank.

Germanus raised his hand in a blessing as the stout man knelt before him. The men of his retinue did the same. They wore iron helmets and knee-length mail shirts, and their horses were of good quality, possibly bred in Gaul or even as far afield as Hispania. Germanus had once been a military man himself, and was quietly impressed. Their master was clearly a man of substance.

"Welcome, Your Grace," said the latter, "we have long awaited your coming. I am Aurelius, Consul of the province of Maxima Caesariensis."

AMBROSIUS

Germanus laid his hand on Aurelius' bald head. "The blessing of God upon you," he said distractedly.

So the Britons, he thought, *or some at least, have clung onto their Roman titles. This one styles himself Consul. Self-appointed?*

Aurelius slowly rose to his feet. "This is my son, Ambrosius," he said, nodding at a slender young man kneeling beside him.

Germanus saw little physical resemblance between the two. Ambrosius was no older than eighteen, and already a head taller than his sire, with a sensitive, almost luminous beauty completely lacking in the older man. His eyes were extraordinary, large and blue, a delicate opalescent blue, with long lashes.

There was a flaw in his almost feminine good looks. His nose had been broken, probably in combat, and set awkwardly. The result was ugly, but it was like a crack in an otherwise perfectly rendered stained-glass painting, or a broken tessera in a complex mosaic. It somehow made Ambrosius more interesting.

The bishop hurriedly looked away. He could not afford to be distracted by sinful thoughts, much less lustful ones.

"We are honoured to meet you, Lord Aurelius," he said, "but had hoped to be received by the High King in person."

Aurelius shifted uncomfortably. "Vortigern cleaves to the Pelagian heresy," he replied, "and has withdrawn to his capital at Viroconium, far to the north-west."

"Viroconium?" Germanus frowned, "I thought the capital of this island is Londinium."

"So it is, Your Grace, but Viroconium lies inside the territory of a tribe named the Cornovii. The city is their tribal capital, and the High King their hereditary chief. He prefers to reside there, surrounded by his kinsmen."

Germanus understood. It was the same all over the Western Empire. Former provinces, shaken loose from Roman control by decades of barbarian invasion and internal decay, were falling back to their old tribal loyalties. This Vortigern appeared to be making no effort to stop the rot in Britannia: indeed, he was actively encouraging it.

"We believe he is sheltering the heretic, Agricola," Aurelius added, "and allows him to preach to his subjects."

Germanus flushed with anger. So that was the way of it. Not content with proclaiming his heresy and snubbing the envoys of God, this Vortigern was openly setting the orthodox church at defiance.

"The High King shall soon regret his folly," said Germanus, laying his hand on Aurelius' shoulder, "and if he refuses to recant his heresy, he shall have to be replaced by a true son of God."

The Consul gave a lopsided smile, devoid of any humour. With his bald head and stocky build, Germanus thought he looked rather like the Emperor Vespasian, whose smile had lent him the appearance of straining at stool.

Germanus had little notion of how the Britons chose their High Kings, but the most likely successor to Vortigern was kneeling before him.

Especially since he now enjoyed the support of the church.

5.

Verulamium had not seen so many people for decades. Once an important town and trading centre of the Roman province of Britannia, it had steadily declined in recent years, until large sections of it were completely deserted. Grass grew in the empty streets, and the winds of winter rattled the boarded-up windows and doorways of abandoned houses.

Ambrosius had visited the town many times, and liked to walk alone through its empty, echoing spaces, haunted by ghosts of the imperial past. The cluster of public buildings in the centre were more or less intact, but the theatre to the north-west was little more than a rubbish tip, its orchestra and auditorium buried under heaped layers of domestic refuse.

Some of the larger houses near the centre of Verulamium were still occupied, but much of the rest was waste, untilled farmland and empty, crumbling buildings. The residential quarter in the south-east quarter lay in ruins, with a few people living in slum conditions amongst the dirt and rubble.

The weight of so many dead generations pressed down on Ambrosius as he studied the faded frescoes inside long-deserted houses, and ventured inside the shadowy coolness of pagan temples. On these occasions he felt like an ant, wandering aimlessly among the ruins of a dying civilisation.

But not today. The streets were packed with people, flooded in from the surrounding countryside to catch a glimpse of the Gaulish bishops, and hear them preach. News of the approach of Germanus and Lupus had preceded them like a storm, whipping the dozing populace into a frenzy.

It is like a sickness, thought Ambrosius as he made his way into the forum, hand-in-hand with his little daughter, Morgana. To his left, a pace behind him, walked his wife Helena. Two of his father's soldiers went before the family, bellowing at the teeming crowds to make way, and shoving aside those who were slow to react.

Or a disease.

Ambrosius had never witnessed anything like it. All the way from Portus Adurni, where they landed, the bishops had inspired unheard-of displays of piety among the orthodox faithful. Thousands flocked to see them and listen to the fiery sermons they preached, often by the roadside or in fields, since no church was large enough to contain such a multitude.

"Follow their progress," Ambrosius' father had ordered him, "let the people see you in their company. We must gain as much influence as possible from this."

Aurelius had ridden north, no doubt to indulge in further intrigues with his friends and well-wishers, leaving his son to win the favour of the bishops. And of the Pope in Rome.

Ambrosius knew his father desired to overthrow Vortigern and seize power for himself. Not as High King, perhaps, a title he despised as barbaric, but as a sort of latter-day Roman governor.

"Britannia shall be a Roman province again," Aurelius was fond of saying, "and my descendents shall wear the purple for a thousand years."

Ambrosius tried to be a dutiful son, but felt like a hypocrite, smiling and fawning over the bishops, pretending to be their most fervent supporter, merely for political gain.

He was a devout Christian, and had heard many tales of the miracles performed by Germanus and Lupus in their own country. Germanus, especially, was famous for healing the sick, simply by laying hands on the afflicted person and calling on the saints.

At Verulamium he decided to put Germanus to the test. First he had ridden to Londinium to fetch his wife and daughter, though Morgana was a weak and sickly little creature. Just three years old, she had never travelled so far in her short life.

Ambrosius had overruled his wife's protests for good reason. Their daughter had been partially blind from birth, and her sight was getting steadily worse with age. No amount of prayer, no form of remedy known to British apothecaries, could halt the strange films growing over her eyeballs. Her eyes had become dilated and red-rimmed, the corneas hazy, and she complained of being able to see nothing but vague shapes moving in darkness.

AMBROSIUS

"I will take her to Germanus," Ambrosius told his wife before they left the capital, "he is famed for healing the blind and the lame."

"But she is so weak," protested Helena, "she will have to ride with me in a litter, over rough roads, at the worst time of year. You know how vulnerable she is to colds. She almost died last winter. I could not bear to lose her. Not after…"

Ambrosius held up his hand. He knew what she was about to say. They were a young couple, married when he was just fifteen and she thirteen, and had already lost one child. A boy, who lived just long enough to be baptised before the spark of life flickered out. Ambrosius had longed for a son, but God saw fit to take him away.

"She will not die," he said firmly, "God would not be so cruel. Not again. He brought Germanus here for a reason. I believe he can restore Morgana's sight."

Helena looked unconvinced. "God's teeth, woman, what else can we do?" he cried in exasperation, "if she goes blind, what sort of a future will she have? No man will agree to marry her, unless we bribe him. She will end up a cripple, alone and childless, living out her days in a convent."

He regretted the words instantly. They fell upon his wife like hammer-blows, driving her to tears. Helena's misery only fuelled his determination to take the child to Germanus and wring a miracle out of him.

Now he was nearing the northern end of the forum, a huge open-air square surrounded by a covered walkway, which usually served the town for a marketplace.

Today it was reserved for the bishops. They stood on a raised platform at the northern end, preaching the reality of original sin and divine grace, and calling the wrath of God down upon the heads of Pelagian heretics.

The forum was packed with the faithful, many of them murmuring or shouting in agreement at what they heard. If any Pelagians were present, they were careful to remain silent. Germanus had sent out a constant stream of challenges during his progress from the coast, daring any supporter of the false doctrine to meet and debate with him in public, but so far none had responded.

"Cravens!" Germanus was bellowing, spittle flying from his mouth as he shook his fist at empty air, "well might they hide in their caves and forests, shunning the light! If ever the followers of Agricola showed their faces, they would be burned and blinded, seared black by the fire of truth, yea, and pierced by the lance of God!"

Both he and Lupus exuded charisma, but Germanus was the more forceful of the two, and seemed to enjoy condemning heretics as much as converting them.

From near the foot of the dais, Ambrosius gazed up at the bishop, and found it difficult to believe he had once been a soldier. Emaciated, stooped, his eyes bulging, face purple with effort, tendons straining in the sides of his thin neck, he looked like a starving lunatic.

Still, Ambrosius reminded himself, *he is getting his strength from somewhere.*

No man who ate so little, and denied himself all the comforts of life, should have been able to draw on such furious energy. Germanus slept no more than three or four hours a night, and his entire being crackled with restless, nervous vitality. His colleague, Lupus, was merely drunk on God. Germanus was consumed, a shell of flesh and bone, filled with holy fire.

"Your Grace," Ambrosius cried when the bishop paused for breath, "may I bring my daughter before you? She is sick, and in need of healing."

Germanus glanced down at Ambrosius. He looked startled, and momentarily lost for words. The crowd also fell quiet, but the more devout among them quickly rediscovered their voices.

"Heal her! Let the saint work a miracle! Let God's will be done!"

The bishop seemed to pale a little, and exchanged doubtful glances with his colleague. Ambrosius was surprised at his hesitation, but Germanus could hardly deny the request with so many people looking on.

"Bring her up," he said when the shouting had died down, though his voice lacked something of its previous force.

Ambrosius gave his wife an encouraging nod, and then led Morgana up the short flight of wooden steps onto the platform. A renewed burst of cheers rang throughout the forum, mingled with wild chanting and snatches of psalms.

There was a softer side to Germanus. His weathered face cracked into a smile as Ambrosius presented the little girl, a smaller version of her father, all pale beauty and soft black ringlets.

Morgana showed no fear of the towering, cadaverous priest. She stood perfectly still, as though under a spell.

"Her eyes," said Ambrosius, raising his voice above the din, "there is a film over them. We have tried all manner of remedies, but nothing works."

Germanus didn't seem to hear. He gazed thoughtfully down at the child, his hand fondling the battered little box dangling from a chain round his neck.

A tense silence swept across the forum. Even the most hysterical souls fell quiet, clenched in concentration, willing the bishop to work his miracle.

Still Germanus did nothing. Ambrosius wondered if this was a deliberate ploy, a way of heightening the drama. He glanced down at his wife, whose eyes were fixed on their daughter.

Poor woman, he thought with a twinge of guilt, *our life together has nothing but sadness and loss. I must be a better husband. A better man.*

At last Germanus acted. He lifted the chain from round his neck, and gently pressed the lid of the box against Morgana's eyes.

"This box contains the knuckle-bones of three holy saints," he cried in ringing tones, "they have the power, through the Lord, of healing any malady known to man. Be blessed, daughter of Christ, and let the shadows lift from your eyes."

A few voices yelped "Amen!", but Germanus had not finished.

"In seven days," he announced, "this girl's sight shall be restored. Her eyes washed clean, even as our sins are washed clean by confession and penance."

For good measure he knelt and planted a kiss on Morgana's brow. She had not moved throughout, but now came to life and looked around helplessly for her father, stretching out her hands.

Knowing she could barely see what lay six inches before her, Ambrosius quickly snatched her up in his arms.

"There," he murmured, stroking her hair, "you have received the blessing of the saints."

Morgana burrowed into the crook of his arm, trembling as though she had been struck. Ambrosius winced as the forum exploded with noise.

Germanus raised his pale, skinny arms to receive the acclaim of the people. Ambrosius fancied the shouts were not quite as loud as before. They had expected an instant miracle, but were left disappointed.

Ambrosius and his family returned to their lodgings. Not wanting to requisition one of the occupied houses, he had taken one of the empty dwellings near the forum. No-one had lived here for years, but it was still fit for habitation.

Later, in the privacy of their bedchamber, Helena was not afraid to voice her doubts.

"Seven days!" she exclaimed, "and on the eighth day, I suppose Morgana's eyes will be healed?"

"So the bishop promised," said Ambrosius, "you were there as well. You heard him."

Helena turned away from him. Her slender frame shook, and for a moment Ambrosius thought she was weeping.

"He is playing for time," she said angrily, "the old fraud knew he could not perform a miracle, so he gave himself a week's grace. Long before the seven days are up, he and his fellow charlatan will have quit Verulamium."

"You must not speak like that of holy men," said Ambrosius, shocked by her attitude, "I won't have it. Germanus and Lupus are two of the most famous churchmen of our age. They will likely be declared saints when they die. It is a sin to talk ill of them."

"Saints?" was the bitter reply, "any man can be made a saint, it seems, if he wears a filthy tunic and can mumble a bit of Latin. Perhaps Germanus' knuckle-bones will end up in a little box, so some other tonsured fraud can use them to heal the sick."

Ambrosius was at a loss. Never, in their three years of marriage, had Helena uttered such impious, blasphemous words.

He was briefly tempted to chastise her. His father had never hesitated to raise his fist (or stick) to his mother if he thought it necessary. Husbands were supposed to chastise troublesome wives.

No. The mere thought was ridiculous. Ambrosius had never hit his wife, and wasn't about to start now. He didn't have it in him. It was sorrow, he decided, and concern for Morgana, that made her speak thus.

In the event, Helena was proved right. Germanus and Lupus did leave Verulamium before the seven days were up, but for good reason.

On the second day after Morgana's blessing, a group of noblemen in rich apparel rode into the town, along with their servants and warriors. They came in splendour, war-horns blowing and banners unfurled as they clattered through the streets towards the forum.

"Where are the foreign bishops?" their leaders cried, "where are these so-called holy men? Let them come out, if they have the courage, and talk with us!"

They were Pelagians, come to Verulamium in response to Germanus' public challenge. The bishop and his colleague swarmed out like a couple of angry bees to meet them, and for two days the forum was a scene of furious argument as the opposing parties hurled their contending doctrines at each other, laced with venomous insults and threats of hellfire and damnation.

The citizens flocked to watch the show. Those who couldn't get inside the packed forum waited just beyond the gates, straining to listen to the raised voices inside. Some adventurous souls climbed onto the roof of the covered walkway, and sat with their legs dangling over the edge, watching the men on the platform work themselves up into a fury. It was, many said, the best entertainment Verulamium had seen since the theatre closed down.

Ambrosius did not attend. He was weary of it all, and longed to be in the saddle again, chasing Saxon pirates. His brief taste of action in the skirmish near Branadunum had whetted his appetite for war. There was something gloriously straightforward about it. The excitement of combat, real combat, was akin to no other.

He reminded himself of the cost. The Saxon chief, Wiglaf, had come near to killing him, and left him with a good scar.

Vortigern had forced his father to compensate Wiglaf's kinsmen. Four hundred head of cattle! Even Aurelius, one of the wealthiest landowners in Britannia, couldn't readily produce so many livestock in a short time, so he had paid off the blood-price with half the beasts and thirty slaves. The Consul's pride, as well as his material wealth, had suffered a humbling knock.

Perhaps war is not so grand after all, thought Ambrosius, *I should not desire it.*

War, however, soon came looking for him.

6.

The bishops and the Pelagians continued to rage at each other with undimmed ferocity for another day and all through the night. Germanus, it was reported, took no rest, and stood on his feet for hours on end, shouting down all opposition.

"The man will have a seizure," remarked Helena, "he is driven by passion, nothing else. It cannot sustain him forever."

Ambrosius feared the debate would end in bloodshed, for neither party was willing to yield a step, but then God intervened.

A lone rider cantered into Verulamium on a spent horse, both lathered in dust and sweat. He entered via the western gate, next to the cemetery, and wearily croaked out his tale to the sentries.

Barely an hour after his arrival, the news had spread through the town like fire.

"A horde of barbarians has landed on the coast of Venedotia," one of Helena's slave-girls, who had heard the tale in the street, reported to Ambrosius, "not just a raiding party this time, but an army. Thousands of Scotti and Picts and Saxons."

She wrung her hands. "The pagan races have gathered under a single banner, and mean to slaughter all the Christians in Britannia!"

The girl, a native of Camulodunum, fell to weeping. Ambrosius knew her for a silly creature, much prone to exaggeration, and went out into the street to obtain a less hysterical account.

He eventually got one from the captain of the city garrison, who was holding a council of war at the basilica, a large court building beside the forum.

"He's a man of the west himself," the captain said to Ambrosius, jerking his thumb at the messenger, "of the Cornovii, or so he claims, and an old soldier. Gives his name as Gwri."

Ambrosius ran his eye over the messenger, a short, dark-skinned man with cropped grey hair, punishing a flask of wine. He wore a soiled tunic and braccae, with a woollen cloak clasped at the shoulder, and might have been a civilian if not for the sword-belt at his waist.

The Cornovii were a powerful tribe in central Britannia, with their capital at Viroconium. Vortigern owed his election as High King to the power he wielded as their chief, as well as being chief of the remnants of the Ordovices, a smaller tribe further to the west.

"Where is this barbarian host supposed to have landed?" asked Ambrosius, "all I know is that they are prowling about somewhere in Venedotia."

"The north-west coast, he says," replied the captain, "near Deva. They have the town under siege."

Ambrosius frowned. Deva, the famed City of the Legions, was some twenty miles north of Viroconium. If there really was a barbarian host on the loose, then Vortigern should have marched to deal with the threat.

Deva still had strong walls, but there were no soldiers stationed there anymore. The civilians might hold out for a while, but would soon crumble under a determined assault.

"You," he demanded of Gwri, "tell me about this plague of pagans. What is our High King doing about it?"

Gwri sucked down the last of the wine and wiped his mouth on his sleeve before replying.

"Not much," he replied in a high, sing-song accent, "sitting on his backside, last I heard. I didn't come from Viroconium. I'm a farmer."

"A farmer with a sword," said Ambrosius, nodding at the spatha hanging from Gwri's belt.

"Veteran, see?" the other man replied with a grin, flapping his hand in a mock salute, "did my twenty years' service at Deva, before the legions left. Probably the last legionary in the country, me. British-born. Decided to stay here. Why should I care what happens to Rome? Never even seen the place."

Ambrosius had to smile. In truth, there were plenty of ex-legionaries left in Britannia, most of them natives like Gwri, given allocated plots of land after their terms of service had ended. It was another old Roman policy. Settling retired soldiers close to towns and cities provided an extra measure of security.

"I got my little farm a couple of miles west of Deva," Gwri went on, scratching his unshaven chin, "and saw the sails of the pagan ships before they landed. My neighbours took their families into the town for safety. I got no family. Didn't fancy being cooped up inside Deva listening to painted heathens screaming for my blood. So I decided to ride east and warn people. Do a bit of good."

"Did you warn the people at Viroconium?" Ambrosius asked.

"Aye. Went there first. They wouldn't let me in. Gates closed, archers on the battlements. Vortigern isn't coming out."

Ambrosius was stunned. If Gwri spoke true, a mighty pagan horde was ravaging the country just a few miles north of Vortigern's tribal capital, and the High King would not march out to fight them.

It is his duty to defend the land, he thought, *his sworn and sacred duty. What else is a High King for?*

"Lot of pagans, mind," said Gwri, "biggest host I ever seen. Three or four thousand, easy."

Ambrosius stared at him. "You saw them, with your own eyes? That many?"

Gwri nodded, slowly. Ambrosius was still learning how to judge men, but the old soldier's eyes shone with bleak honesty.

"The High King still has his cavalry," remarked the captain, "five hundred horse. The barbarians have nothing to match them. Just a few spearmen on hill-ponies. A few determined charges would sweep the whole lot into the sea."

"If led by a determined man," said Ambrosius, "not a coward."

He stopped. It was all well and fine, throwing around accusations of cowardice, but someone was going to have to lead an army against the pagans: assuming any kind of an army could be scraped together from the scattered British garrisons.

Ambrosius had little idea how far news of the invasion had spread, or how the various local governors and magistrates might respond. They would more than likely follow the example of the High King, choosing to cower behind strong gates and high walls while barbarians rampaged over the countryside.

His father, Aurelius, was the only other man powerful enough to muster an army. He was either in Londinium or touring his vast estates. Ambrosius wasn't sure which. If the latter, then no message would reach him in time.

"Sir," said the captain of the garrison, "what should we do?"

He and his subalterns looked nervously at Ambrosius, waiting for him to respond.

Ambrosius ran a hand through his thick black hair. He was still fearfully young, just eighteen, and these men expected him to devise a plan of campaign on the spot. They were all significantly older than him, but mere limitanei, garrison troops, while he was the son of the Consul.

"Send a rider to Camolodunum," he said, trying to sound decisive, "my father may not be there, but most of his cavalry are stationed in the old legionary fort. Their commander is to bring them west, without delay, to join us on the march to Deva. We will have left Verulamium by then, so he will simply have to find us on the road."

"We?" replied one of the subalterns, "there are no more than forty men in the garrison, including the cooks. We can't march out to face the enemy alone!"

"The town is currently stuffed with people," Ambrosius reminded him, "including hundreds of able-bodied men. Some of them will take up arms and join us. We can collect more troops on the way. Fear nothing. My father's buccelari are worth many times their number of dirty savages."

They still looked frightened, but had enough residual sense of duty – and respect for Aurelius – to do his bidding.

While they mustered the garrison, Ambrosius returned to his lodgings to bid farewell to his family. It was a short walk from the basilica to the house, but the street was crammed full of people, pushing and shoving as they streamed towards the forum.

He sighed as he fought his way through the heaving mass of bodies. No doubt Germanus was due to give another performance.

Someone jostled against him, knocking him against a wall. Ambrosius cursed, and almost retched as the raw stench of the man hit him in the back of the throat. He was not only unwashed, but barefoot and unshaven and clad in a tattered old gown, tied at the waist by a length of rusting chain.

A flagellant, thought Ambrosius. One of those Christian fanatics who wandered the country, mortifying their own flesh and preaching the word of God to anyone who cared to listen.

"The holy Germanus will lead us to victory!" hollered the flagellant, "he shall be our Gideon, and the blessed Lupus shall be our Joshua!"

Others took up his cry. Baffled, Ambrosius pressed his back flat against the wall and waited for the surge of humanity to pass by.

The entrance to the forum was to his right. A great roar split the skies, and Ambrosius looked in that direction to see Germanus emerge, standing on an oval shield held aloft by two burly citizens.

Germanus wielded a spear, and had donned a helmet over his filthy cowl. Another citizen walked behind him holding aloft a crude banner made of a square of red cloth tied to a pole. Lupus, ever the more circumspect of the two, walked quietly beside the standard bearer, looking slightly embarrassed.

"Germanus! Germanus!" the mob chanted, pumping their fists in the air, "Germanus shall lead us!"

Slowly, it dawned on Ambrosius what was happening. Germanus had once been a soldier, before God summoned him to the priesthood, and had not forgotten his old life.

Ambrosius struggled through the crowds, back to his lodgings, and spent the evening deep in thought. Outside, the joyous screeching of the mob echoed through the streets long through the hours of darkness.

His wife and daughter joined him in the triclinium, where the Romans who used to dwell in the house had taken their meals. Once a gorgeously decorated room, with luxurious couches and frescoes on the wall depicting forest scenes, it was now cold and dingy, with damp rising up the walls. The frescos, made by painting directly onto wet lime plaster with watered pigment, were still remarkably intact, as was the mosaic on the floor.

Elsewhere in the house the mosaic was in bad repair, and crudely patched with mismatching tessarae.

The hypocaust or underfloor heating system had not been used for many years. It was partially collapsed, so Ambrosius ordered one of his slaves to lay a fire in the middle of the floor.

"Open a window to let the smoke out," he ordered, "otherwise we'll choke to death."

Light was provided by a horn lantern inside an iron cage, hanging from a hook on the ceiling. Ambrosius and his family huddled around the fire, seated together on a long bench his slaves had dragged in from one of the rubbish heaps littered about the town, and ate a frugal meal of bread and cheese.

Morgana sat between her parents, staring mutely into the spluttering flames. The slaves had piled up a heap of dry kindling inside a ring of stones, and lit it with flint and tinder. The wood burned well enough, but cold air drifted in from the open window.

Huddled up inside his cloak, Ambrosius coughed and shivered, and wished himself back in Londinium. His father's house was an old Roman villa, and possessed all the civilised comforts (including a working hypocaust) that were slowly falling out of use in the rest of the country.

"Listen to those poor fools," said Helena in a low voice, "like a lot of sheep, bleating in celebration of death."

It was dark outside, and the decaying streets of Verulamium rang to the sound of hundreds of voices lifted in song. The wild chanting of earlier had faded, replaced by an orderly procession of psalms. Ambrosius thought it akin to being trapped inside the nave of a gigantic cathedral.

"The bishops have won," he said, rubbing his hands for warmth, "this invasion has united everyone, Pelagians and Christians, under the banner of the church. Fear is a wonderful unifier."

He gently draped his right arm over Morgana's shoulders, and drew her close to him. The slave sent to look for firewood had returned with news that Germanus and Lupus were hard at work re-baptising Pelagians, dipping their heads inside a stagnant pool of water beside an old well. Those men who had ridden into Verulamium, arrogantly calling for the bishops to come and face them, were now eager to be re-admitted to the orthodox faith.

"Useful spear fodder," he muttered, and was surprised at his own cynicism.

"What will you do?" asked Helena, turning to face him. She was a plain girl, with an oval face, sad brown eyes and chestnut hair, parted in the middle.

Helena was the only daughter, by a British mother, of Lucius Septimius, governor of Camulodonum. Ambrosius' father had arranged her marriage to his son as part of a political alliance. In return for gaining the second most powerful man in the country as a brother-in-law, Lucius agreed to supply horses, fodder and arms to Aurelius' cavalry, and keep the old legionary fort they used for a base in good order. He also agreed to support Aurelius in council against Vortigern.

Ambrosius tried his best to love Helena, but felt more pity than affection. Childbirth, and the loss of their son, had aged her, but the recent spark of anger was something new. Once he had recovered from the shock of his wife's blasphemy against Germanus, Ambrosius was intrigued.

"I won't serve under the bishop," he replied, "we need an army to repel the pagans. He is gathering a rabble. Germanus will lead all of them, men, women and children, to their deaths. The Picts and their allies may be Godless savages, but they can fight. What does Germanus hope to do, frighten them away by singing a few hearty psalms? The man used to be a soldier!"

He shuddered, and not just with the cold. The singing outside was getting louder.

Helena stroked her daughter's hair. No matter how she tried to comb or smooth them out, Faustinia's mop of curls was unconquerable.

"If you stay behind," she said, "men will call you a coward. I care nothing for what men say, but you do. So does your father."

"I'm only staying behind to wait for my father's cavalry to come up from Camulodunum," he replied, "once they arrive, I will lead them west, on the heels of Germanus' mob."

She looked up in alarm. "I thought you said you would not serve him?"

"Nor will I. But he can't fight the invaders alone. I will shadow him, and lead my cavalry against the enemy host when needed."

"With luck, and the grace of God," he added, gazing into the fire, "they will be enough to turn the tide."

Helena said nothing, but laid her hand on his knee. Ambrosius drew much comfort from her touch, and the warmth of the little body at his side.

7.

The next morning Germanus led his makeshift army out of Verulamium, a straggling horde of soldiers and citizens, beggars, squatters, priests and country folk, with the bishop and his colleague striding to the fore. Crude banners waved over their tonsured heads, roughly stitched or painted with the symbol of the cross.

As their followers flowed out of the ruined town, they sang a ragged Te Deum, though some of the less pious souls to the rear added a few blasphemous and downright sordid verses of their own making.

Ambrosius stood on the steps of the basilica and watched them depart. The captain of the garrison and his subalterns had also stayed behind, though over two-thirds of their men had succumbed to the air of feverish piety that hung over the town like an unhealthy vapour, and gone with Germanus.

Gwri, the veteran of Devo, stood beside Ambrosius. "I make about fifteen hundred," he said, "mostly farmers and townsfolk. A dozen horsemen, and maybe one spear between three."

"The Picts are also ill-armed," said Ambrosius, reaching for a sliver of comfort.

Gwri gave him a slow, appraising stare. "You ever fought the Picts, lad?" he asked, "or even seen them?"

"No," Ambrosius admitted, "but my father has. He says their warriors fight naked, and are covered in tattoos. They believe the tattoos contain some kind of magic which protects their bodies in battle."

"There's a bit of truth to that. A bit. Some of their young warriors fight naked – sky-clad, they call it – in honour of their gods. They don't have much metal either, their country being so poor, so only the richest chiefs carry swords. Don't be fooled. A flint or bone-tipped spear can do just as much damage as steel."

His eyes took on a distant look. "Me, I've killed more Pictish raiders along our northern coasts than I can remember. Faced a few of their war-bands in battle. They still use chariots, like our

47

ancestors used to ride into battle against the legions. See a line of chariots rattling towards you, followed by naked warriors screaming like devils, their bodies smeared in tattoos, hair spiked with dung, waving spears and axes, and tell me they are ill-armed."

"That's not all," he added cheerfully, "they got plenty of missile troops. Slingers, bowmen, javelin-men. Crossbowmen, too. Simple weapon, the crossbow, and slow to load, but can punch through leather armour at short range. The Picts use them for hunting."

"There's also the Scotti to reckon with. Vicious bastards. Maybe a few Saxons as well, with those double-handed axes and horrible long knives they carry."

"But we have God on our side," said a pale subaltern, who had grown steadily paler as Gwri spoke.

The veteran sniffed. "I heard men call on God in the heat of a fight," he said quietly, "didn't stop them getting their limbs chopped off, and bleeding and shitting themselves to death."

Ambrosius would have rebuked Gwri for his blasphemy, but the words died inside him. The old soldier had seen much death and suffering, and knew what he was talking about. God's ways were unknowable. He was not there to be summoned at will, like some kind of divine genie. Men could pray, if they wished, but prayer had to go hand-in-hand with practicality.

His messenger had gone to Camulodunum, some twenty miles to the east, the previous afternoon. When Germanus and his army of the faithful had marched out of sight, Ambrosius made his way to the eastern gate, past the ruins of a triangular-shaped temple, to watch for the arrival of his father's soldiers.

He stood on the parapet over the twin archways of the gate, which was built of stone and flanked by two horseshoe-shaped towers. Unlike much of the rest of the fortifications, the gate was in good repair, and usually manned by a sentry. Most of the garrison had marched off to death or glory with Germanus, so Ambrosius was alone.

It was a mild day, and he stood leaning against one of the towers for the best part of an hour. A light breeze snatched at his cloak. The road stretching away before him led south-east, straight to Londinium. His father's men, assuming they heeded his summons, would most likely follow a side-road from Camoludunum before turning onto it.

While he waited, Ambrosius' mind filled up with dark thoughts. Most of them centred on his daughter, and Germanus' failure to heal her. The seven days were almost up, yet Morgana's sight showed no sign of improvement.

Her father's worst fears were coming to pass. She would live out her days as a cripple, unwanted and unloved by all save her parents, and die in a convent.

Ambrosius' own eyes stung with tears. He angrily wiped them away. Aurelius was right. He was too soft. The fate of Britannia hung in the balance, and here he was, wallowing in grief.

At least Morgana will never go hungry, he told himself, or want for a warm bed, and a roof over her head. How many helpless peasants have the Picts and their allies butchered or enslaved? How many women and children have died? Rome has abandoned us. Now the legions have gone, only the wealthy and powerful can defend the people of this country.

Only me.

It was a startling thought, and occurred to him just as his eye caught the glint of spears, advancing rapidly up the road.

A long line of horsemen rode into view, and his heart leaped when he recognised the battered features of their officer: Menas, the old decurio who had helped Ambrosius in his first fight against the Saxons.

"Two hundred men!" said Ambrosius when the horsemen had cantered through the gates, "I didn't expect half so many. Did the envoy I sent find my father?"

"Yes, sir," replied Menas, "Aurelius happened to be in Camoludunum, staying with the governor, when your message arrived. He gave the order for his men to come and join you here. Two hundred and forty, to be exact. The remaining sixty were either out on patrol, or needed by Aurelius for his personal guard."

Ambrosius frowned. "Why did he not lead his men here personally?"

"I couldn't say, sir. My duty is to follow orders, not interpret the meaning behind them."

He didn't need to venture an opinion. Ambrosius had already thought of a reason for his father's absence. Aurelius was deliberately staying away to give his son a chance to distinguish himself in battle. Thus he avoided embarrassing and angering Vortigern – the High King would not bear to be shown up as a coward by his greatest rival – and advanced the reputation of his family.

If I succeed.

"How far to Deva?" Ambrosius asked Gwri, while the buccelari rested and stabled their horses in what remained of a military compound in the north-east quarter.

"Eighty miles, more or less," the veteran replied, "a four or five-day march for regular soldiers. More like a week for Germanus and his merry band. Deva might have fallen by then."

"It might have fallen already," Ambrosius said grimly. He knew little of the true situation in Venedotia. All he could do was plunge into the unknown.

He bade a tender goodbye to his family. Helena held him close, but had to guide Morgana into her father's arms.

Ambrosius knelt to study her eyes. They were still clouded and bloodshot, more so than ever, and the irises hideously swollen.

"Can you see me, child?" he asked gently, "can you see your father?"

Morgana gave a little shake of her head. "Just shadows," she whispered.

"So much for the blessing of the saints," Helena said bitterly, "so much for the power of the holy Germanus."

Ambrosius was suddenly filled with anger, but didn't know who to direct it against. Germanus, his wife – even God?

He led the buccelari out of the western gate at a measured trot. His intention was to shadow the pilgrim host without making it aware of his presence. Germanus' piety was only equalled by his arrogance, and he would insist on taking command of Ambrosius and his men.

"His followers will start drifting away once the excitement has worn off," said Gwri, "they won't get halfway to Ratae, let alone Deva."

The old soldier had volunteered to come along. Ambrosius found his presence reassuring, even if he did talk too much, and tell the most outrageous lies about his exploits on the battlefield.

The presence of veterans like Gwri and Menas at his side helped to strengthen Ambrosius' fragile confidence. He was painfully aware of his youth and inexperience, and the unaccustomed responsibility weighed heavily on him.

His men made slow progress along the dilapidated Roman highway leading to Ratae, and at times Ambrosius made them lead their horses on foot. He wanted to keep men and beasts fresh, as well as avoid catching up with Germanus.

He sent Menas ahead with a troop of scouts, ordering them to report back every evening.

"Looks like you were wrong," the veteran said on the third evening of the march, smiling at Gwri, "Germanus is gaining men, not losing them. His numbers swell with every town and village he passes."

A friendly rivalry had sprung up between the two old soldiers, the Roman and the Briton. Ambrosius was amused by it, and wondered if they were competing for his favour.

They were now in the land of the Catuvellauni, another ancient British tribe subjugated by the Romans. Germanus was apparently ignorant of tribal boundaries, and attracted all men to his banner.

"How many does he have now?" asked Ambrosius.

"Some two thousand," Menas replied, "farmers, mostly, but a few country nobles have joined his ranks, and brought their warriors with them. Supplies are pouring in. Oxen, sheep, goats. Wagonloads of fresh bread, flitches of bacon and barrels of ale."

"The pagans still outnumber them two to one," said Gwri, "most of those silly peasants will run away as soon as they catch a whiff of the Picts. Not to mention the women and children. Some use they will be."

Gwri's cynicism grated on Ambrosius' nerves, and the sight of Ratae did nothing to cheer him. Once an important town in the heart of Roman Britannia, though not as large as Verulamium, it had also fallen into ruin and decay.

Ambrosius knew that Ratae had been gutted by a fire, back when his father was a child. No effort had been made to rebuild and restore the smoke-blackened public buildings in the centre of the town. The forum, basilica and market hall lay empty and silent. Nearby lay the public baths, also deserted, and a row of large stone houses. Possibly a few squatters still dwelled in the houses, and the ruins of the poorer settlements near the river, but otherwise Ratae had become a town of ghosts and shadows.

We are crumbling away, Ambrosius thought sadly as he gazed upon the walls of the fort, built just outside the town walls, *tumbling into darkness. Only the light of Christ guides us now.*

Where was Christ leading them? To slaughter and catastrophe. Somewhere in the distant, rain-soaked forests of the north-west, where even the legions had feared to tread, an army of painted savages lay in wait. Ambrosius pictured them lying in wait among the trees, more like beasts than men, and shivered.

From Ratae they followed the highway that led to the High King's capital at Viroconium, before turning north towards Deva. Germanus would have to follow the same route, and Ambrosius found it difficult to believe that Vortigern would not be shamed into action, once he saw the host of ragged pilgrims shuffling past his gates.

All kinds of uncertainties tumbled through his mind. Perhaps the invaders had moved on to besiege Viroconium, by far the largest occupied town in the west, after overrunning and destroying Deva. Or Vortigern had finally remembered his courage, and marched out to face the invaders in the open.

Or perhaps he means to sit inside his city, and wait. For what? For the pagans to march east, burning and plundering, until my father is forced to confront them?

AMBROSIUS

The devious ways of the High King's mind were beyond him. Perhaps Vortigern was doing nothing in the hope that the Picts would kill Aurelius. Then, with his nearest rival safely disposed of, he could ride out at the head of his five hundred cavalry and smash the barbarians. None would dare challenge his power then, the saviour of Britannia.

Ambrosius meant to give Viroconium a wide berth, and took his men into the wild country several miles east of the city, hoping to pick a route through the hills and forests before returning to the highway.

They were camped in the woods at dusk, beside a fast-flowing stream, when Menas rode in to make his nightly report.

"The gates remain closed," he said, "Germanus stood outside and shouted for Vortigern to come out, begging him to join the army of Christ, but got nothing save insults from the sentries, and a shower of rotten vegetables. The High King has chosen to hide behind his walls. Not even God's messenger can pry him out."

"I rode a few miles north," Menas added, "skirting the highway, so none of Germanus' crowd would see me. There is fire in the north. The land is burning."

Ambrosius swallowed his bit of dried meat with difficulty. Gwri hadn't exaggerated, then. A sizeable pagan host really had landed, and was busy destroying everything in its path.

His men broke camp at dawn, just as the skies started to lighten, and quietly led their horses on foot through the woods. Ambrosius lacked a guide, but Gwri had some knowledge of the land, and by mid-morning they were on the highway again.

Ambrosius could see the smoke for himself now, rising over the rolling hill country to the north, and the great cloud of dust marking the progress of Germanus' host.

He halted on a ridge. Here the land to his left swooped down to a ravine hacked into the deep forest below, while the highway continued to carve a straight path over the hills, leading down to a bridge spanning a wide expanse of river.

Beyond the bridge lay the fortress-city of Deva. It lay some two miles to the north, and was still intact. No smoke rose from

53

the neat rows of houses and public buildings inside its stone walls, nor was there any sign of the barbarian host.

"Look there," said Gwri, pointing his spear to the west, beyond the river. The gaunt hills clustered thickly in that direction, rising in places to form mountains, their peaks obscured by mist.

The dust-cloud was moving west, south of the river, towards the mountains. Ambrosius spotted fires glimmering near the summit of one of the highest peaks.

"Beacons," he said, "Germanus must have seen them too."

He looked to Gwri and Menas for advice. "I agree," said the decurio, "the pagans have abandoned the siege and withdrawn into the forests. Perhaps they saw Germanus coming, and assumed it was a proper army marching to the city's relief."

"Their delusion won't last long," said Gwri, "look at those fools! They should have taken refuge inside Deva and thanked God for their deliverance."

It was the eve of Easter. Ambrosius wiped the sweat from his face, and reflected this was a fine time to witness the slaughter of Christians.

Whatever else he might be, Germanus was no coward. He had spotted the fires on the mountain, assumed the pagans were somewhere near, and led his army of impending martyrs straight towards them.

Ambrosius quickly spied out the land. A range of smaller hills lay to the south-west, their slopes carpeted with pine forest. Germanus' army, now visible as a long, trailing mass of tiny figures, like so many toy soldiers, was advancing towards some flatter ground north of the hills.

"To the forest," he said, "we'll stick close to Germanus' flank."

The older men made no objection, and he led his cavalry at the canter down the shallow, grassy slope curving down to the edge of the woods. As they neared the edge of the trees, Ambrosius thought he heard distant singing – psalms again! – and, beyond that, on the very edge of hearing, the ominous throb of war-drums.

It was hard going in the woods, for the trees were densely packed and the ground difficult. Stumbling and cursing,

AMBROSIUS

Ambrosius dragged his horse on foot up the hill, with his men strung out in a long line behind him. At least he had a good view of the land to the north, which dipped into a wide valley before rising to meet the mountains.

When he reached the highest point, Ambrosius stopped and peered down at the eastern edge of the valley. Just over a mile away, Germanus had halted his army on the high ground overlooking the dip. From this distance, it was impossible to see what they were doing, but the hills echoed to the sound of plainchant. It sounded like they were holding an Easter service.

Ambrosius shook his head. Madness. He patted his horse's neck and reached for the flask of water at his belt.

His hand froze on the stopper. The thumping of drums had suddenly grown louder, almost in time to the beating of his heart. He looked to the mountain, rising to the west, and saw the fires near its peak were moving.

Moving down, towards the valley, at a terrifying pace. He counted twenty lights – no, thirty, forty – flowing down the mountain-side.

Then the forests near the foot of the mountain exploded with noise. Braying war-horns, mixed with high-pitched shouts and frenzied drums.

The Picts burst from the trees. Hundreds of painted and tattooed warriors, just as Ambrosius had envisioned them in his nightmares, screaming as though they were on fire, naked berserkers to the fore, brandishing stone axes and horn-tipped spears.

They had spotted the Britons march into view on the other side of the valley, Ambrosius reasoned, and saw they were no soldiers. Elated at the prospect of an easy victory, followed by a feast of slaughter, the Pictish chiefs had unleashed their young warriors.

"No chariots," remarked Gwri, who appeared calm as ever, "difficult to ferry them across the sea, I expect, especially in those pathetic little boats the Picts use. Christ, listen to them wail!"

No chariots, but a few score horsemen, warriors mounted on tough little hill-ponies. These led the charge, though their comrades on foot were almost as fast, swarming across the valley floor like a gigantic pack of wolves, howling for blood.

"There," said Gwri, pointing his spear at a band of spearmen loping out of the woods in the wake of the horsemen, "Scotti. Pirates from Hibernia."

Ambrosius found them difficult to tell apart from the Picts. To him, they were all barbarians: tattooed, screeching, blood-maddened savages.

"Mount!" he shouted, hurling himself into the saddle. The ground before him fell away steeply, but was less thickly wooded to the north-west, and he could risk leading his men down at the trot. Once they reached the bottom, they could fall on the Picts while the latter were making chopped liver of Germanus' holy fools.

Did he have enough men to turn the tide? Ambrosius had no time for doubts. He turned to his bugler and barked the order to advance.

The bugle was drowned by a deep-throated roar from the east, thousands of impassioned voices bellowing a single word:

"HALLELUJAH!"

The word bounced and reverberated off the hills, and the echoes had barely died away before it was renewed: *"HALLELUJAH!"*

And   again:
"HALLELUJAH!"

Ambrosius turned his head to the east. He picked out Germanus, towering over the other tiny figures beside him, waving his skinny arms in the air. His troops, if they could be called that, were frantically waving their spears and banners. Those without merely shook their fists or knelt in prayer. It seemed that Germanus had gathered his followers on the edge of the ridge and ordered them to shout at the heathen.

It had some effect. The wild charge of the pagan host faltered. Many of their warriors stopped to look around in confusion at the surrounding hills, evidently fearing they were about to be attacked from all sides.

"HALLELUJAH!"

As the echoes of the fourth shout bounced back and forth, it was joined by the call of a bugle, sounding through the dark forests to the south. A single horseman charged out of the trees, followed by two more, and then a flood of red-cloaked mounted soldiers.

Seeing the barbarians hesitate, Ambrosius had seized the moment and led his men down the slope at a gallop. His horse stumbled and slid on the uneven ground, and at one point almost pitched him from the saddle, but he managed to keep her upright.

Ambrosius charged out onto the valley floor and steered his horse towards one of the Pictish banners, a crude affair made of a piece of skin – Ambrosius wondered if it was human – stretched tight over a cross-bar and crudely daubed with the image of a snarling wolf's head. The banner was mounted with a skull, definitely human, and a cluster of Pictish warriors stood under it.

"Kill their chiefs," Ambrosius remembered his father telling him, when he was growing up and learning the arts of war, "barbarians are like sheep. Once the shepherd is down, they quickly scatter."

The weight of his spatha felt good in Ambrosius' hand. He knew Gwri and Menas were close behind him, guarding his flanks. The rest of his men were fanned out in a long line behind the standard bearer, and free to pick their own targets.

"Hit them hard," his father's stern voice echoed inside his memory again, "and hit them fast. The barbarian peoples are fierce in battle, but if you can withstand their initial fire, it soon splutters out."

He saw the Picts were scattering, panicked by the booming shouts of "Hallelujah!" and the sudden appearance of the British cavalry. Only the pick of their warriors stood firm, screaming at the lesser men in the harsh Pictish tongue.

The warriors under the standard uttered a great shout and bounded towards Ambrosius, led by a tall man in a heavy plaid cloak, wielding a spear in both hands. He wore no shoes, and his arms were bare, displaying intricate swirling patterns of blue tattoos inked into his pale flesh.

He stabbed at Ambrosius, who wheeled his horse to the right and took the thrust on his shield. The spear-point scraped harmlessly against the wood, and he swung downward, over the rim of his shield, aiming for the Pict's unprotected head.

His opponent was quick, and caught the edge of the spatha on his spear. The thin ash shaft snapped clean in half, leaving him holding two broken bits of wood. Ambrosius struck again, and this time the edge of his blade cut deep into the Pict's head, cleaving his skull in half and drenching his long, carefully combed red hair in gore.

Another warrior lunged screaming at Ambrosius, stone axe whirling in his hand. Again Ambrosius blocked the wild blow with his shield, though the force of it threw him off-balance. Before he could recover, Gwri thundered in and thrust the tip of his javelin into the axe-wielder's neck, impaling his white throat.

The standard bearer stood his ground, eyes bulging as he shrieked insults at the Britons. Ambrosius spurred towards him, but Menas was already there, hacking downwards with his spatha. The Pict had no shield, or any armour at all, nothing save for a loincloth, and could only defend himself with his axe. He fell to the ground, blood pumping from the neat gash Menas had opened in his neck, and the grisly standard fell with him.

Ambrosius paused to gulp in air and look around him. Everywhere the barbarians were in flight, fleeing for the safety of the woods. Ambrosius' horsemen gave chase, spearing and cutting them down like rabbits, but then another deep-throated shout rolled across the valley floor.

He twisted in the saddle, and saw Germanus' rabble charging down from the ridge. The skeletal figures of the bishops led the attack, waving iron-shod cudgels – churchmen were forbidden to deliberately shed blood, so could not carry edged weapons in combat – filthy robes hitched up to the knees, exposing painfully skinny white legs.

Behind them surged the army of the faithful, roaring out their war-cry over and over again until it made Ambrosius' head ache.

AMBROSIUS

"HALLELUJAH! HALLELUJAH! HALLELUJAH!"

He watched in a kind of daze as Germanus' followers went to work. They fell upon the fleeing Picts like savage dogs, tearing them to pieces, showing no trace of pity or mercy. Now they were the barbarians, their thin veneer of civilisation stripped away, revealing the horror beneath.

Some of the things Ambrosius witnessed in that reeking valley of death stayed with him for the rest of his days. He saw a young woman, her long black hair dabbled with blood and bits of flesh, shrieking wordlessly as she straddled a fallen Pict and hacked at the back of his neck with a sickle. Elsewhere two boys, no older than nine or ten, laughed as they stabbed out a warrior's eyes with their little knives. A horse had ridden over him, and he was unable to fend them off, his body broken and mangled by the churning hoofs.

For a couple of holy men, Germanus and Lupus proved adept at slaughter. Between them, they accounted for over a dozen enemy warriors. Ambrosius watched Germanus gleefully clubbing to death a Pictish chief, who had two broken legs and was begging for mercy, and felt his gorge rise.

The brief battle was over, but the massacre continued for hours. Ambrosius' cavalry pursued the fleeing enemy into the woods, where some of the barbarians turned and made a stand. There were scattered outbreaks of fighting, but the fervour of the Christians swept all before it. Hundreds, if not thousands, of pagans were killed, victims of the avenging fury of God.

Eventually the pursuit slackened off. The survivors vanished into the woods and mountains, leaving great piles of their dead strewn about the valley floor. A heavy rain started to fall, washing away the stench and taint of blood.

"Victory," said Gwri, who was wiping his bloodied sword on a piece of rough cloth torn from a corpse, "a messy victory, like none I ever seen, but still a victory. God was with us after all."

Ambrosius wearily removed his helmet. A mist was slowly billowing across the valley, stealing in from the mountains to the west, and the stench of blood and death was in his nostrils.

God had won the day. How could it possibly be doubted? A few lines from scripture crept into Ambrosius' head.

"Now let God arise," he murmured, "and may his enemies be scattered; may his foes flee before him. As smoke is driven away, so drive them away. As wax melts before the fire, so let the wicked perish before God."

A faint cry of "Hallelujah" drifted across the valley, rising above the groans and screams of the dying. Ambrosius dismounted, laid his helmet to one side, and was violently sick.

8.

"Listen, you sack of wine," growled Aurelius, his deep voice echoing around the rotunda, "my son may be young, but he has already killed more barbarians than you have in over thirty years."

His finger stabbed like a spear at the man he had termed a sack of wine: Cadeyrn, King of the Durotriges, a tribe dwelling in the south-west of Britannia.

Cadeyrn flushed. An old man, lost somewhere in his mid-fifties, he did indeed have the look of one who liked to douse his liver in strong hot wine. His plump, raddled face was a ghastly shade of puce, and he was so fat and ridden with gout he had to be carried about in a chair by a team of perspiring slaves.

When he swelled with anger, as he did now, Cadeyrn looked in serious danger of exploding.

"I'll not listen to your insults, you jumped-up cattle thief!" he bawled, "I am a king, and my ancestors were kings while yours were still grubbing a living from the soil! Farmers, that's what they were, jumped-up tin merchants – slaves, too, I should imagine!"

Aurelius' thick-lipped mouth curled into a sneer. "King of what?" he retorted, "some petty tribes in the arse-end of Britannia. I hear your warriors don't even obey you, but make war on each other as they please, while you sit farting and sucking down mead in your hall."

The accusing finger stabbed again. "Five times the Saxons have raided your lands in the past year. Five times! What have you done to stop them? They murder your people or carry them off as slaves, burn their villages, take their livestock. I ask again, what have you done to stop them, lord king?"

His heavy fist crashed down onto the table. "Nothing!" Aurelius roared, "and there lies the problem. Men like Cadeyrn lack the soldiers and the courage to defend their own turf. How long can we continue to exist, unless we work together to defend our own borders?"

This was too much for Cadeyrn. His face grew redder and redder as he struggled for words, and at last he turned to the High King.

"Lord king, order him to apologise," he quavered, "or I shall quit this council and never return!"

Vortigern thought the King of the Durotriges sounded like a spoiled child.

"Stay where you are, Cadeyrn," he said grimly, "not that you can move anywhere without the help of your slaves."

Cadeyrn spluttered. "I…I demand…I shall…"

"Be silent."

This time his voice cracked like a whip, and the obese man wisely stayed quiet.

Vortigern was in no mood to be trifled with. He locked gazes with Aurelius, and wished he had the power to strike men dead with a glance.

Even if he wished to, Vortigern could not force the Consul to apologise. He didn't have the power to make him do anything. Not anymore. Not since Aurelius' whelp, Ambrosius, had played his part in the stunning victory over the barbarians near Deva.

Vortigern had badly misjudged the situation. When word reached him of the landing of a huge pagan host in the north, he decided to remain inside Viroconium. Not through fear (or so he told himself) but to wait for the pagans to break up into smaller war-bands, as they always did when sated with plunder. Then he intended to ride out at the head of his buccelari and crush each band in turn.

He hadn't expected the pestilent foreign bishops, Germanus and Lupus, to whip up thousands of civilians and country folk, and lead them against the enemy. Nor had he expected Aurelius to give his son enough men to rescue Germanus' rabble from almost certain disaster.

The Hallelujah victory, as it was called, had brought glory to Aurelius and his family, and nothing but shame to Vortigern. Germanus and Lupus had departed in a haze of glory, back over the Narrow Sea, but the damage was done. They left the High King clinging onto power by his finger-nails.

He felt the stares of his fellow councillors drilling into him. The majority had quietly shifted their support to Aurelius, leaving Vortigern with just four or five staunch allies he could count on. Even those only stayed loyal because they were Pelagians, and feared what might happen if an orthodox Christian mounted the throne.

Even so, Vortigern would not go down meekly into the dust. "Whatever the flaws in our defences," he said, as firmly as he dared, "there can be no question of restoring the comitatenses, or the office of Comes Brittanarium. I see no advantage in hanging on to these old Roman titles."

He spread his hands. "My lords, Rome has deserted us. She deserted us over twenty years ago. The Western Empire is falling to pieces, and will never be restored to its full glory. How long must we ape Roman customs? Rome is the past."

His words met with murmurs of agreement from his handful of allies. Vortigern's disparaging references to Roman customs were meant as a deliberate insult to Aurelius, who was notoriously proud of his Roman heritage and distant kinship to Saint Ambrose of Mediolanum.

To Vortigern's disappointment, the insult failed to sting. For once Aurelius kept his quick temper in check and mustered a calm response.

"On the contrary," he said, lacing his thick, powerful fingers together, "Roman offices, especially military offices, should never have fallen into abeyance. What have we replaced them with? Nothing. I have been made responsible for the defence of the Saxon Shore, even though Consul is a civilian title. We rely on foreign barbarians to protect us. The forts are stuffed with Germanic mercenaries, and more of their foul kin arrive on our shores every month."

He looked pointedly at Vortigern. It was no secret that the High King was now employing Saxons in large numbers, and giving them land in return for military service. It was another reason for his growing unpopularity.

"As for the Wall," Aurelius continued, "it steadily rots away, and we do little to re-man the deserted forts and outposts. What use is a barrier, eighty miles long, with so few troops to defend it? The Picts climb over the abandoned stretches of wall and raid at will. How long before they realise we lack the means to fight them, and decide to invade in force?"

"The recent invasion was a near thing, and only staved off thanks to the favour of God and the actions of a few brave men, including my son. It should never have come to that. As soon as word of the landing reached us here in the south, we should have had a mobile field army ready to ride north and destroy the threat."

"Agreed," said Lucius Septimius, Aurelius' brother-in-law, "the victory was nothing short of a miracle. Without the intervention of the blessed Germanus, as well as the undoubted courage of young Ambrosius, God knows what might have happened. The whole of Venedotia might have been lost, swallowed up by the pagans."

Vortigern's loathing was now divided equally between Aurelius and Septimius. The governor of Camulodunum was a thin, fussy little man, a civil servant to his finger-bones, and put the High King in mind of a rat. An ambitious rat, mind, with sharp teeth and claws.

Lucius' speech met with approving noises, and a few of the councillors went so far as to applaud. Stymied, Vortigern could think of nothing to say.

"I propose we put it to a vote," said Aurelius, "the office of Comes Brittaniarum to be resurrected, and the title bestowed on my son. He is to be given command of not less than a thousand troops, horse and foot, to be based here in Londinium."

Vortigern clenched his jaw. *Comes Brittaniarum* was one of the old military offices created by the Western Empire for the defence of Britannia. The comitatenses was the Roman term for the field army, composed of the best troops available and used as a mobile defence force, able to march at a moment's notice to deal with any threat to Britannia's defences.

In contrast, the limitanei of the Saxon Shore and elsewhere were mere garrison troops, local levies given basic military training and usually fit for nothing save guarding the walls of towns and cities.

Whoever commanded the comitatenses wielded enormous political as well as military power. The last Comes had departed from Britannia with the legions, and Vortigern deliberately neglected to fill the void. He wanted no over-mighty subjects, poised to challenge his authority.

The thought of Aurelius' son in charge of the best fighting men in Britannia was enough to bring him out in a cold bath of sweat. Ambrosius was still just a boy, not yet twenty, and heavily influenced by his father. Through him, Aurelius would command the only standing army in Britannia, and possess the means to destroy Vortigern.

"Cast your votes," said Aurelius, "all those in favour, raise your hands."

Eighteen hands went up. Vortigern glared furiously at their owners. He would see them cold and dead, he vowed, if it took him fifty years to do it.

The High King derived his power from the council, and could not countermand a majority vote. Otherwise Vortigern would have happily called in his guards – Saxons, most of them – and ordered them to butcher his opponents in cold blood.

At times like this he envied the Caesars of old, who wielded supreme authority and brooked no opposition. The likes of Caligula and Nero would have long since thrown Aurelius to the lions.

"All those against," said the Consul, smiling in triumph at Vortigern. A few useless hands went up, but the High King's was not among them. Instead he desperately racked his brains for a counter-argument.

"Ambrosius is too young," he said weakly, "yes, he distinguished himself at Deva, but should we really entrust our security to an eighteen-year old? If we are to have this army, led the command be given to some older, more experienced man."

A flash of inspiration hit him. Maybe he could persuade the council to give command to Guechta, the Saxon chief of his personal guard. Guechta owed Vortigern everything, and would happily follow his orders.

It proved a vain hope. "How old was great Alexander when he won his first victories?" said Aurelius, "besides, my son will have enough veteran officers about him to guide his steps."

His words were echoed by another storm of approval. "British officers," he added, gazing at Vortigern through narrowed eyes, "loyal to the council, and to the High King."

To you, Vortigern thought bitterly*, and those lickspittles around you.*

The battle was lost, but he was too proud to stop fighting. "Comes Brittaniarum is a meaningless title," he said doggedly, "unless we restore the others as well. Who will serve as the Dux Brittaniarum, or Comes Litoris Saxonici? Ambrosius' wife, perhaps?"

This raised a few sniggers from his allies, but Aurelius batted aside the feeble jest. "The actual title need not concern us overmuch," he replied, "if Comes does not suit, then we can create another one for Ambrosius."

"I have it," said Lucius, snapping his fingers, "Dux Bellorum. All the military offices combined into one."

Dux Bellorum, or Leader of Battles. Aurelius nodded, and clapped his brother-in-law on the shoulder.

Vortigern quietly seethed. The precious pair had obviously anticipated his objections before the council, and cooked up their answers beforehand.

Leader of Battles. And who will his battles be fought against?

That evening, after the council had dispersed, Vortigern vented his rage on the furnishings in his bedchamber.

"Traitors!" he screamed, hacking savagely at a couch with his sword, "conspirators! I'll see them all hanged – boiled alive – torn apart!"

His wife, Sevira, quietly sat on her couch with her hands folded, waiting for the storm to settle. She was slightly younger than her husband, nearing thirty-six, and still a beauty at first glance. Closer study revealed the lines of exhaustion around her eyes and mouth, and the thin strands of silver in her dark brown hair.

Sevira had borne her royal husband three sons, and endured his passions for over twenty years of marriage. The effort had drained her, reducing her to a shadow of the vivacious girl she had once been. Vortigern rarely shared her bed these days, preferring to slake his lust on younger, more exciting women, but he still valued her company and advice.

When the couch had taken sufficient punishment, he turned his attention to the wall hangings, throwing away his sword and tearing at them with his bare hands. Roaring and gnashing his teeth, he threw the tattered bits of rich fabric onto the floor and stamped on them until his anger was spent.

He turned, panting and sweating, to his wife. She returned his gaze without a trace of fear in her eyes.

In the fledgling days of their marriage, he had often taken his fist to her during his drunken rages, and enjoyed it. The beatings stopped when she climbed into his bed one night and pressed the edge of a dagger to his scrotum.

"Mark me again, and I will mark you for life," she hissed into his ear, pressing the cold steel a little harder against his wilting flesh, "the High King must have sons, but you will lack the tools to make them. Britannia shall have a gelding for a ruler."

If she had been anyone else, Vortigern would have put her aside and chosen a more pliant woman for his consort. Sevira, however, was the only living child of Magnus Maximus, remembered by British poets and storytellers as Macsen Wledig – Maximus the Emperor.

Maximus was almost the last of the ambitious governors of Britannia who aspired to an imperial crown. He had revolted against the Western Emperor, Gratian, and crossed the sea to Gaul to press his claim, taking most of the British garrison troops with him. Like most pretenders, he came to a bad end, slaughtered in Dalmatia by the forces of the Eastern Emperor Theodosius, along with his men.

Despite the catastrophic end to his career, Maximus was remembered as something of a tragic hero in Britannia. His family still enjoyed a degree of wealth and prestige, and Vortigern's marriage to Sevira had proved a useful step on his way to securing the title of High King.

"If you have quite finished your tantrum," she said, "perhaps we might salvage something from the mess you have created."

Frowning, he looked around at the ripped-up hangings and mangled couch.

"Not the furniture," she added impatiently, "I meant Aurelius. You cannot let him have his army. It would mean the end of you. Of us. Our family."

"You don't have to tell me that," Vortigern growled.

He reached down to pick up his sword. "How I yearn to have this at his throat," he said, weighing the blade in his hand, "Lucius as well, and Flavius Sanctus, and all the others who have turned against me."

He glanced around at their bedchamber. It suddenly seemed mean and shabby and ill-lit, barely fit for a peasant, never mind the most important man in the country.

The couple were lodging in one of the largest villas inside Londinium, not far from the old imperial palace. Vortigern hated the palace, with its oppressive Roman architecture and air of gently fading grandeur, and refused to sleep there.

A villa was also easier to defend. Ever wary of assassins, Vortigern had surrounded the place with thirty of his Saxon guards. He almost pitied anyone who tried to get past these big mercenary warriors, magnificent and terrifying in their shirts of gleaming ring-mail, large round shields and burnished helms. Every one carried a stout ash spear, wickedly curved long-axe and the long knife the Saxons called a saex. Vortigern had bought their loyalty with land, and trusted in their greed to keep him safe.

"A ruler should rule," said Sevira, rising, "and beholden to nobody."

She gently took his free hand and led him towards the couch, like a handler leading a trained bear.

Vortigern laid aside his sword and permitted himself to relax, sighing as she started to knead the thick, knotted muscles of his shoulders. No-one, not even the most expensive and best-trained slave masseurs, could ease the tension out of him like Sevira.

"A ruler should rule," she repeated, whispering the words softly into his ear.

Vortigern closed his eyes. "What can I do?" he mumbled, "Aurelius has won, damn him. The council has swung behind him. That boy of his…"

"Do away with him. Do away with them both. There are plenty of blades for hire. A sharp knife, a dark night…"

Her words were smooth as honey, deadly as poison. "Not so easy," he said, pushing her away, "they are both well-guarded. Aurelius goes nowhere without his buccelari."

"Then they will continue to defy you," snapped Sevira, her voice suddenly hard, "and grow in power. As they wax, my husband, so shall you wane."

She slapped him, a sharp, stinging blow across his bearded cheek. "What of our sons? If you care nothing for yourself, think of them. Once you are dead, do you think Aurelius will allow them to live?"

Vortigern rubbed his cheek. His wife's fingers dripped with heavy rings. There would be a livid bruise later.

He had already thought of their sons. Vortimer, the eldest, was nearly sixteen, and quite capable of looking after himself. Catigern and Pascent were still boys. Vortigern needed to survive, if only for a few more years, until they were men grown.

"There will be civil war," he said gloomily, staring at the palms of his hands, "it is inevitable."

"A war we must win," Sevira replied.

Vortigern almost smiled. It was not difficult to picture her leading the troops into battle, riding a chariot like some ancient warrior-queen, her long brown hair flying loose about her.

The High King's own taste for war had soured over the years. In his youth he had fought like a devil, slaying all his rivals for the leadership of the Cornovii in single combat, and then leading bloody raids into the lands of neighbouring tribes. He had made himself the most feared and powerful war-chief in the island, the obvious choice as High King.

Those days were far behind him now. Vortigern had ruled for the best part of eighteen years. He was getting old. His enemies could sense it, and were slowly gathering for the kill.

He shook himself. A flicker of his old warlike spirit remained, and he was not done yet. Far from it.

"Aurelius is building an army," he said, "so I shall do the same. When the time for battle comes, we shall be fairly matched."

Sevira laid her head on his shoulder. "Where will you get the soldiers, my love? There are scarcely enough men left in Britannia to fill two armies."

We have the likes of your father to thank for that, he almost retorted, but thought better of it.

"From across the sea," he said, glancing at the door. Outside, he knew, two burly Saxon gesiths were standing guard. A few hundred such men would sweep aside any native infantry Aurelius could put in the field.

"Mercenaries?" Sevira's voice was full of doubt. "You would use an army of foreign hirelings against your own people?"

"If it comes to it."

He shrugged her off and got to his feet. Yes, an army of Saxon mercenaries. With them at his back, he could rule unchallenged. A true High King at last, with no snivelling councillors to restrain or betray him.

"The people of this land are like wild dogs," he said, "and must be whipped to heel."

9.

Under cover of night, three keels slid like sharks up the gateway to the Tamesis. There was no wind, and their oars gently plashed through the darkened waters.

Each of the keels was crammed with Saxon warriors, and well-furnished with battle-gear, coats of mail and bladed weapons. All young men, eager for loot and land, they had taken the swan's path, risking the voyage across the broad northern seas from their lands in the far north of Germania.

They were led by two nobles, brothers named Hengist and Horsa. The brothers sailed in the largest keel, and stood together at the ring-whorled prow as the moonlit shores of Britannia glided past either side of them.

Hengist was the smaller of the two, and the younger. Just twenty, he had long grown tired of the dreary, sheep-infested flatlands of his own country, and listened avidly to the tales of Britannia brought back by his kinsmen: of the richness and variety of its land, and the generosity of its ruler, who stood in dire need of warriors to fill his armies.

"Home," he said, gazing at the gently undulating folds of the landscape as they drifted past. He stood with arms folded, legs placed wide apart, as sure-footed aboard deck as he was on land. Like many of his people, Hengist had been a sea-rover since he was old enough to ply an oar.

Horsa bristled into life. He was a giant of a man, almost seven feet high, and wore a wolfskin cloak over his mail. He had killed the wolf himself, strangling the beast with his bare hands. The fearsome reputation he enjoyed in his homeland was built on such feral acts of violence.

"Our home lies across the broad swell of the sea," he said in his deep, guttural tones, "we have no roots here."

Hengist slowly shook his head. "I will never go back," he murmured, "never."

He drew in some deep breaths. The air was pure, and imbued with the salt tang of the sea. There was good soil in this country, ripe for tilling. He could smell it.

Here I shall have my steading, he thought, *and raise a litter of bairns. In time I shall die and be buried in the good earth, with my sword and shield.*

First, the good earth had to be prised from the hands of its owners. Hengist had little fear of the Britons. They had grown weak under Roman rule, and forgotten how to fight.

Vortigern was the key to unlocking the riches of Britannia. Back home, Hengist had carefully listened to descriptions of the High King from those who had served under him. A great warrior in his day, he was growing old, and increasingly hated and despised by his own people. Unable to command their loyalty, he surrounded himself, like some feeble latter-day Emperor, with a strong guard of Germanic mercenaries.

Any ruler who lost the love of his people had only a short time to live. Hengist's own father, Wictgils, a minor chief among the Angles, had been betrayed and murdered by men who once warmed themselves by his hearth and called him lord.

His sons had dutifully avenged his death. Hengist lost an eye in the battle, though it was really a bloody skirmish, with less than a score of warriors on either side. After the fighting was done he and Horsa had cruelly tortured the survivors, before leaving them tied to stakes in the winter-bound forest for wolves to eat.

This spate of bloodletting gave rise to the usual blood-feud, but Hengist had little desire to pursue it.

"Why stay in this poor country," he had said to his brother, "fighting like rats to defend our father's damp hall, when there is good land over the sea begging to be taken?"

Horsa would happily have stayed, to kill until he was killed in his turn, but had learned to respect his brother's wisdom. Horsa was no great thinker (Hengist privately considered him incapable of thought) while the younger sibling had inherited the full share of their mother's agile brains.

Hengist made use of those brains now. Britannia may be a treasure-house, waiting to be plundered, but it was not entirely undefended. Shortly before leaving his homeland, he had heard dark rumours of a new power rising in the island. A remnant of Roman military might, led by a shadowy figure named Ambrosius Aurelianus.

"Ambrosius," he muttered under his breath. Some old soldier, no doubt, left behind after the legions abandoned the country. The power of Rome was dying fast, but a few embers sparked here and there. They needed to be stamped out.

"When will we land?" complained a female voice, interrupting his thoughts, "I am sick of this boat, and the stink of men."

The voice came from under a pile of furs at the base of the keel's single mast. It belonged to Rowena, Hengist and Horsa's sister. Pale moonlight glinted on her golden hair as she shifted uncomfortably under the furs and stretched out one delicate white arm to stifle a yawn.

Hengist's eye fastened on her. She was a treasure beyond price, with which he meant to entrap Vortigern.

"Not long now, sweet sister," he said softly, "soon your backside will be resting on soft cushions instead of rough timbers."

She sniffed. "I have a chill. I don't like this country. It's too cold and damp. Just like home. You said it would be pleasant here. You *promised*."

Hengist ignored her. He had listened to Rowena's whining for most of his life, and learned to treat it like a background noise, akin to the soft rustle of rain on the thatch of his father's hall.

"Be quiet," growled Horsa, who lacked his brother's patience, "unless you want a split lip."

Hengist placed a calming hand on the other man's brawny forearm. He had always been the peacemaker in the family.

"Enough," he said, "Horsa, you will not lay a finger on our sister. She is of little value to us covered in bruises."

Horsa shrugged his massive shoulders, and turned back to the prow. Rowena was of little concern to him. She was the only one of four sisters to live to adulthood. The other three were buried beside their mother, inside a tumulus on a bleak headland overlooking the sea.

"Women," he grunted, "good for nothing but cooking, fucking, spitting out bairns and dying."

Hengist smiled. As always, he knew better.

Their keels eventually ground ashore on the western bank of the river. Hengist's knowledge of the layout of Britannia was sketchy, but he knew that Londinium lay some miles to the west. The broad river continued to twist and turn in that direction, as far as he could see by the light of the moon, and apparently cut deep into the heart of the island.

"Best to land in some secluded spot," he advised his brother, "before we run into the British outposts."

As the eldest, Horsa was the chief of the tribe, and had to make the final decision. "I don't see why," he grumbled, "Guechta sailed right up to the walls of their city and demanded the blood-price for Wiglaf. He got it, too."

Guechta, captain of Vortigern's personal guard, was their cousin. It was he who sent word back to the land of the Angles, informing his kin of the riches to be found in Britannia.

"Guechta took a risk," said Hengist, "the gods favoured him that day, but I prefer not to tempt them."

Horsa took a little more persuading, but Hengist knew how to work the levers of his brother's unsubtle mind. Eventually he agreed to land, and the keels glided to shore, just before a pronounced bend in the river. They were shallow-draught vessels, ideal for sailing up narrow rivers and waterways, if somewhat fragile on the open sea.

The Saxons disembarked in silence and carried the boats into the marshy ground beyond the river.

Hengist knelt in the shallow, murky waters and dug out a handful of wet mud. He raised it to his face, licked it, and smeared some on his cheeks, like war-paint.

"Mine," he murmured, looking around at the reed beds and the dark, impenetrable mass of trees, "all mine. My land. My turf."

The Saxons advanced some way inland, and spent an uncomfortable night in the forest, sheltering under the trees from the incessant drizzling rain.

AMBROSIUS

"Water from the gods," Hengist remarked cheerfully as he sat with his back against a gnarled oak, tilting his face up to catch the drops, "gives life to the earth. We should be grateful."

His men looked anything but grateful. The rise of the sun heralded a bleak dawn, and the brothers rose to lead their grumbling, sleep-derived followers west, towards Londinium.

Hengist wanted to see something of the land he had come to conquer, and insisted on continuing on foot. The Saxons left their keels hidden on the edge of the marshes under piles of reeds. If danger threatened, they could always beat a path back to the river, and hence to the sea.

The forest reminded him of the dark, troll-haunted wastes of his homeland. After a time he found himself wondering what manner of native sprites lurked among the foliage.

A clever man, Hengist was still as prey to superstition as any of his folk, and sweat prickled on his skin as his fearful imagination conjured up all kinds of horrors: dog-headed demons with the bodies of men; writhing, snapping, fire-breathing serpents; the malicious spirits of warriors who failed their lords in battle, doomed to wander the earth as ghouls, hungry for the blood of the living.

Rowena was also affected. "This is the underworld," she sobbed as she stumbled over the rough ground, flanked by two of Hengist's best warriors, "you have brought me to Hel."

All in all, Hengist was glad when the nightmarish forest started to thin out, and he caught glimpses of green fields and pastures stretching away to the west.

The Saxons halted when they reached the edge of the woods. Horsa sent a runner ahead to spy out the land in case there were any British soldiers prowling about.

The Britons were known to use cavalry, darting in to throw javelins from horseback before wheeling away, beyond the reach of spears and axes. Saxon warriors almost always fought on foot, and were nervous of encountering bands of horsemen in the open.

"Nothing ahead save a deserted steading," the runner reported when he returned, "I searched the house. It's deserted."

Horsa tossed the lad a bracelet for his trouble – as chief, he was expected to be liberal in the giving of rings and other precious items – and led his men out of the woods.

They advanced up the slightly rising ground beyond in close order, ready to close up and form a shieldwall at the first hint of danger. Every man wore a helm and ring-mail byrnie, and carried a long spear and oval shield. A few carried long-axes in place of spears, and all carried saexes hanging from their belts.

The steading came in sight over the brow of the hill, a wattle-and-daub longhouse with smoke rising lazily from a hole hacked into the matted thatch on the roof. Some sheds and outbuildings were scattered around the house, and a sheep-pen. The pen was empty, but a few chickens scratched and pecked in the dirt, and the lowing of a cow sounded from inside one of the larger sheds.

"Thought you said it was deserted?" Horsa growled at the runner, pointing his long-axe at the smoke.

The youth paled. "It is, lord. There was a fire in the hearth. The people must have fled in a hurry and left in burning."

Horsa let his axe drop and stood still for a moment, beetling brows stitched together while he glared at the farmhouse.

Cursing his brother's sluggish mind, Hengist ambled up to his side and gave him a sharp elbow in the ribs.

The big man came to life again, and turned to look at the warriors crowded behind them.

"You, Ceawlin," he grunted, picking out a lanky, red-haired man with a ragged stump where his left ear used to be, "what do you reckon to this place?"

Ceawlin's blue eyes took in the house, the outbuildings, and the thirty or so acres of fertile green pasture that surrounded them. Lush woodland bordered the fields in every direction save west, where the river flowed on through low-lying meadows.

"Good grazing land for cattle, lord," he replied warily, "a man would do well to settle here."

"Glad you like it. It's yours."

Ceawlin's eyes widened, and one of his mates grinned and gave him a slap on the back. A few of the others scowled, but their turn would come. There was plenty of land to go around, and Horsa was as generous as he was brutal.

Hengist was pleased. His brother had done well. Of course, Ceawlin would have to kill the British peasants who owned the farm, assuming they ever came back, but that should present little difficulty. Though young, all the men of Horsa's war-band were seasoned killers.

His mind briefly dwelled on Vortigern. The High King of the Britons might own the land, but he seemed keen to throw it away, like good grain from a sack. With luck, he would approve Horsa's gift to Ceawlin in return for military service, and all the other gifts to follow.

They splashed through the watery meadows while a light mist descended, rolling across the bleak landscape. The view ahead was obscured, but the Saxons were born adventurers, and had no fear of the unknown.

Hengist strained his eyes to see through the murk. He had heard countless tales of Londinium, its sheer size and grandeur, and was eager to see if the reality matched up to his dreams. His father's wooden hall was big enough to house and feed maybe a score of warriors. Londinium, according to the stories, was a vast enclosure ringed by walls and towers of stone, containing many thousands of souls.

He could neither read nor write, and struggled to count beyond thirty. He could barely imagine such an ocean of humanity, and had never set eyes on Roman fortifications. His heart thrilled at the prospect. Here was the place for a man of ambition. A land begging to be taken, conquered and re-forged.

The thump of hoofbeats sounded in the mist. Hengist stopped, and raised his spear as a signal to halt.

At a growl from Horsa, the Saxons closed up, ready to form a ring of shields. Hengist twisted his head to look for Rowena, and was relieved to see her standing behind the line of warriors. She was capable of defending herself, if need be, and gripped a saex in her right hand.

He listened carefully to the hoofbeats. Two, maybe three riders.

Their outline gradually became visible in the mist. Seconds later they emerged, three horsemen in red-dyed cloaks and leather tunics, their bodies protected by round shields and steel helmets with nose-guards and dangling cheek-pieces. They carried light throwing javelins, and long swords in cross-bound scabbards hung from their belts.

Their horses were white, chestnut brown and a dappled grey. The man on the white was in the lead, and appeared to be their officer.

He was careful to rein in a spear's throw from the Saxons, and regarded the band of warriors without any fear on his leathery, clean-shaven face.

"We saw you coming up the river yesterday," he said, "why did you not sail on to Londinium? You would have received a warm welcome."

Hengist exchanged surprised glances with his brother. The officer was a Saxon, or at any rate spoke the Saxon tongue fluently.

Horsa seemed lost for a response, so Hengist answered for him. "We thought to approach the city undetected," he said, "in case we were taken for a band of pirates and attacked."

The officer smirked. "Small chance of that. I was a pirate myself once, until Vortigern gave me a villa and a troop of horse. Oh, and a British wife to go with them."

"I assume," he added, shifting his grip on his javelin, "that you have come to offer your services to the High King?"

Hengist could have laughed. Was it really going to be this easy? Most farmers shot wolves when they threatened their herds. Vortigern was inviting the wolves in and offering them a place by the fire.

"Yes," he said when Horsa again failed to speak, "we wish for nothing more in the world."

10.

After five years in charge of the comitatenses, the man who led them had grown into a very different creature. His mother's influence had faded with age, and more of his father's harsh character was shining through. Ambrosius was still handsome, in a cold, hard-faced sort of way, and had acquired an air of stern confidence absent in his younger self.

Whenever duty allowed, he still liked to walk alone among the visible ruins of Britannia's past. One mellow autumn evening found him wandering among the shadows of the massive ring of stones, two miles west of his new headquarters.

He came here as often as possible. The place fascinated him, and served to fill his mind with a necessary sense of awe after a long day of military drill and exercises.

Contained inside a ditch, the stones had been erected by long-dead hands in two concentric circles. The inner cluster was formed of five massive pairs of uprights, each pair capped by a lintel, while the outer cluster consisted of about thirty smaller uprights, also with lintels.

Several of the latter sets had fallen down, and lay on their sides like fallen giants, crushed by the inexorable weight of time. Other stones of various shapes and sizes were scattered outside the outer ring of the henge, their original purpose a mystery.

Whenever Ambrosius came here, he made a careful count of the number of stones. He did the same this evening.

"Forty-two," he said aloud, resting his back against the large, flat stone that lay in the middle of the central cluster.

The number was always different. This time there were three less stones than his previous visit. Ambrosius found the phenomenon both eerie and exciting.

As a good Christian, he knew he should avoid this place, a monument to ancient pagan beliefs and rites, but there was a kind of peace here.

Ambrosius contemplated all the long centuries that had passed since this place was built, and the men who dragged or ferried the various pieces of bluestone and sandstone that made up the circle. Those ancient labourers were nothing but dust now, lying in forgotten graves.

He suddenly remembered what he was leaning against, and pushed himself away.

His knowledge of Britannia before the Romans came was limited, but he knew the pagan sun-worshippers of old had practised human sacrifice. The central stone, or altar-stone as he thought of it, was probably where the sacrificial victims were strapped down before having their hearts cut out.

Sometimes, if he knelt beside the stone and laid his ear against it, he fancied he could hear distant screams, echoing down the corridors of time.

He shivered. It was getting dark, and the blood-red orb of the sun was setting over the western hills. The dying light silhouetted one hill in particular, a man-made hump in the landscape, crowned with timber ramparts.

Ambrosius heard the faint call of a bucina, summoning the garrison to their evening meal. He walked to the western edge of the henge and stood leaning against one of the uprights for a time, gazing with satisfaction at his new stronghold.

Mons Ambrius, he called it, or the Hill of Ambrosius. Naming the place after himself was a vain act, but he had planned and overseen its construction. The soldiers who garrisoned it were his. His family resided there. He had the right to call it what he liked. Ambrosius had learned to be assertive, and conceal his natural modesty under a mask of confidence, bordering on arrogance. Modesty was all very fine in a priest, but not much use to the Dux Bellorum.

Not constructed, he reminded himself, *re-fortified. Mons Ambrius rests on the shoulders of dead men.*

The earthwork upon which his fort stood was ancient, and may have been thrown up at about the same time as the stone circle – perhaps by the same people.

It was one of several old hill-forts in the region. There were two more to the south, another two to the north, one to the east and one to the west. Together they made up a formidable network of defences. Ambrosius had placed smaller garrisons in all the surrounding forts, with the main force quartered at Mons Ambrius.

His horse whinnied. He had left her tied to one of the fallen lintels, and she was growing impatient.

"Best we were off," he said, glancing back at the ominous silhouette of the altar-stone, "this is no place for the living after dark."

He suddenly whipped around, alerted by a sound like distant thunder. It was coming from the east.

The land in that direction was flat and featureless, and despite the growing dark Ambrosius was able to see for some distance. His eyes were sharp – as sharp as Menas' had once been – and he picked out a troop of horsemen, galloping hard across the plain. The dragon banner flapped at their head.

Ambrosius clucked his tongue. He hated to see horses treated so cruelly. No doubt they were remounts. His father would have already ridden the first set to exhaustion and left them to die on the road. Aurelius was growing ever more stubborn as he grew older, and refused to appreciate the proper value of good horseflesh.

Aurelius and his men were heading straight for the fort. Their breakneck pace suggested they brought fresh news from the east.

"Old fool," he murmured, and jogged over to untie his horse.

He was in no hurry, and rode back at an easy canter. The days of scrambling after his father's shadow were long gone. Aurelius was still the head of the family, but his son was the real power now. With age and responsibility had come independence, and Ambrosius no longer suffered himself to be treated like some callow subaltern.

The landscape he rode across contained some of the best farmland in the country. It was dotted with villas and farmsteads, and the broad fields, stretching away as far as the eye could see in every direction, were covered in rich crops of golden wheat and barley, almost ripe for harvesting.

Ambrosius halted before the gateway of the palisade on the southern outer bank and hailed the sentry. The squat gate tower was made of timber, and the wooden ramparts flanking it buttressed with piles of dressed masonry, plundered from an abandoned Roman village a couple of miles to the south-west.

"Welcome, lord," cried the spearman on the battlements, "your father is here."

Ambrosius nodded, and waited patiently while the wooden gates were unbarred and swung inward. He urged his horse through the gateway, exchanging salutes with the guards, and up the steep track leading to the inner rampart.

This was also defended by a gate tower and wooden walls, enclosing the perimeter of the hill. The fort was shaped like an arrowhead, steadily narrowing at the northern end. The double line of walls were surrounded by defensive ditches, dug out centuries ago by the original inhabitants.

When Ambrosius first came here, he had set his men to work clearing the ditches of weeds and rubbish. Their spades had turned up all kinds of litter, including flint arrow-heads, pieces of worked slate, smashed bits of pottery, and thousands of animal bones.

No graves, though, for which Ambrosius was profoundly thankful. The notion of desecrating the last resting-places of the dead, even pagan dead, was abhorrent to him. He reckoned a cemetery probably lay near the fort, but had no desire to go looking for it.

The roots of Britannia lie here, he often told himself, *the blood and marrow of the land.*

Ambrosius was descended from purely Roman stock, but his family had dwelled in Britannia for over three generations. Their blood had watered its soil. The defence of the land was his duty.

He reached the summit of the fort, a broad plateau containing storehouses, barrack huts, stables and a smithy, and a timber hall.

Ambrosius handed the reins of his horse to one of the guards, and walked towards the hall. This was a long, rectangular building, built on the foundations of an earlier one. The entrance faced south, with gables at the eastern and western ends, a thatched roof and plastered walls. It was a crude sort of dwelling, especially for one used to the comforts of a Roman villa, but good enough as temporary accommodation for soldiers.

He hadn't counted on his wife, Helena, insisting on living here, and on bringing Morgana with her.

"I shall live by your side," Helena had stubbornly informed him, "as a wife should live with her husband. We cannot leave our child behind."

Ambrosius would have preferred them to live in Camoludunum with her father, instead of a rough military camp, but she brushed aside his objections.

"We share everything in this life," she declared, taking his hand, "including the hardships."

There was no question of them staying in Londinium. The capital was no longer safe, since a state of undeclared war now existed between the High King and Aurelius.

Ambrosius had evacuated his family soon after he acquired command of the field army, along with all his slaves and other movable possessions. Vortigern had seized their property inside the capital, the villas and shops and houses, and parcelled them out to his own supporters.

The doorway to the hall stood open, and warm yellow light flooded out from inside. Ambrosius could hear raised voices, his father's chief among them.

He stepped inside and was almost instantly folded in Aurelius' embrace.

"My God, lad," his father cried, pounding him on the back, "it's good to see you. Six weeks since we last set eyes on each other!"

His hot breath carried a strong whiff of wine. Ambrosius glanced over his father's shoulder, and saw a flagon and two cups standing on the table standing on a raised dais at the western end of the hall. Light came from a fire burning inside a ring of stones in the middle of the floor.

The eastern end was divided from the rest of the hall by a curtain of purple silk. Behind the curtain was Ambrosius' bedchamber, the only private space in the entire fort. His wife and daughter also slept there. They should have come out to greet him, but Helena had chosen to stay behind the curtain. There was little love between her and Aurelius.

"Father," he said, disengaging and holding the older man at arm's length, "I am glad to see you too."

Aurelius had brought ten of his buccelari for an escort. They stood stiffly to attention in a line to the left of the table, their helmets tucked underarm.

Ambrosius briefly ran his eye over them. Good men, with good gear and horses, wasted in the barracks at Camulodunum.

He sometimes contemplated asking his father to give him command of the buccelari. They were some of the best-trained and equipped cavalry in Britannia, and Aurelius had no need of three hundred men for a personal guard. Camoludunum was well-defended, and its walls could easily hold out against anything Vortigern might throw at them.

He couldn't bring himself to do it. Much of his father's pride was invested in his precious cavalry, which he had raised and equipped himself. Rather than cause the old man pain, Ambrosius chose to let him hold onto them.

"You're too soft-hearted, boy…"

Ambrosius recalled the words. They were from his previous life, a half-forgotten time, already slipping into the mire of the past.

"Come," said Aurelius, gripping his son's wrist and leading him towards the dais, "let us drink together. I've already slaked my thirst a little, but not enough." He winced theatrically, and rubbed the small of his back. "Getting too old for these wild dashes, back and forth across the country," he grumbled, "but it couldn't be helped."

"You might have sent a messenger," Ambrosius said mildly, allowing himself to be led.

The flagon on the table was brimful of red wine. Aurelius had almost certainly liberated it from one of the storehouses containing rations for the garrison.

"Your health," he said, handing a cup to his son before greedily swigging down the contents of his own.

While they drank, Ambrosius studied his father. Every time they met, Aurelius had grown a little thicker around the waist, his heavy arms and shoulders a little more bowed. There were fresh lines carved into his jowly features, and the stubble on his chin was grey.

An old dog, Ambrosius thought affectionately, *with a few more barks and snaps left in him.*

Aurelius belched, and wiped his lips with the back of his hairy forearm. "I had to come in person," he said, "I got a message from one of my agents in Londinium, not two days ago. Vortigern is moving west."

Ambrosius' heart beat a little faster. This was it, then. After five years of waiting and planning, the long-awaited war had finally come.

Christ be thanked, he thought. Ambrosius was sick of the false war, smouldering like a peat fire, of digging trenches and erecting fortifications and waiting for Vortigern, who in turn stayed in Londinium and built up his own power.

"He wants the harvest," Aurelius continued, "all the crops in this part of the country."

"For his mercenaries?" said Ambrosius. His father nodded.

"The lands in Cent aren't enough to sustain all the Saxons he has brought over. Over six hundred warriors, along with their wives and families. Think of it! The barbarian filth have already gobbled up all the crops on the treaty lands Vortigern gave them, and are demanding more, like a pack of starving wolf-cubs. He needs to find provisions before winter comes on, or they may revolt and plunder Londinium."

Ambrosius and his father had anticipated such a move from Vortigern, which was why the west country had their troops all over it. Mons Ambrius and the surrounding forts were ideally placed to block any advance along the highway from Londinium, as well as driving a wedge between the High King, his tribal heartlands around Viroconium, and his ally Cadeyrn in the south-west.

"He hasn't marched yet," said Aurelius, "or at least he was still at the capital when I left Camoludunum. Hengist won't let him

tarry   for   long."
The wine had warmed Ambrosius, but the name of the Saxon war-chief caused a chill to steal over him. Hengist was a shadow, a mysterious presence looming behind Vortigern's throne, exercising a malign influence over everything the High King did.

Ambrosius cursed the day Vortigern had taken Hengist and Horsa into his service. The brothers were by no means the first landless Saxon mercenaries to offer him their swords, but none had got so close to Vortigern, or manipulated him so effectively. Horsa was said to be a brute, strong as a bear and about as intelligent, but Hengist was something else entirely. Sly, devious, ruthless, a mind to be reckoned with.

"Are the rumours true?" Ambrosius asked, "has Vortigern put aside his wife for Hengist's sister?"

Aurelius poured himself another ample measure of wine. "He would like to," he replied with a shrug, "but Sevira won't go without a fight, especially not in favour of some plump Saxon wench. And her sons support her, or at least Vortimer and Catigern do. Pascent stays at court with his father, even though he loathes the Saxons as much as his brothers."

"Hengist, they say, won't part with Rowena without obtaining a hefty bride-price for her. Namely, the whole of Cent."

"If Vortigern continues with his follies," said Ambrosius after a brief silence, "he will destroy himself, without any intervention from us."

"Perhaps. But not yet. Hengist is still content to play the loyal servant. He will persuade Vortigern to march west with all the troops he can muster. When that happens, you must march out to oppose him."

"What of your cavalry?" demanded Ambrosius, "three hundred of the finest horse-soldiers in the land, and you have left most of them in Camulodunum!"

Aurelius was unruffled by the note of anger in his son's voice. "Of course. Vortigern also has his spies. He would have been quickly alerted if I moved out in force. We left Camulodunum after nightfall. With luck, none of his agents saw me go. I will ride back at dawn."

AMBROSIUS

Ambrosius stared into the other man's deep-set eyes. It didn't take much perception to read the thoughts behind them. Civil war loomed, and his father had abdicated all responsibility for its outcome.

To him.

11.

Vortigern shivered. His mail shirt felt too heavy, and his helmet too close-fitting. Many years had passed since he last rode to war in person. He had almost forgotten the cold and the discomfort, and the constant gnawing of fear.

Of all the men on the field, he had the least cause to be afraid. He was guarded by sixty of his buccelari, every one of whom was prepared to die before allowing an enemy to come anywhere near the sacred person of the High King.

They were hand-picked, taken as boys from his tribal lands and given the best equipment and training. Vortigern rarely felt secure anywhere, but the presence of these hard-faced soldiers, unbreakably loyal to their king, was a comfort.

He would have preferred to bring all five hundred of his buccelari, but the majority were needed in Londinium. While he marched west to face Ambrosius, their task was to guard his rear, and watch for Aurelius' troops making a sudden dash from Camulodunum. If that happened, they would ride out and intercept the enemy.

Vortigern had left his youngest son, Pascent, in charge of the garrison at Londinium.

Not my youngest son, Vortigern thought angrily, *my only son. The others have broken faith. They are nothing to me now.*

As ever when he thought of his sons, an invisible knife twisted inside him. Vortimer and Catigern had chosen to take their mother's side, and gone with Sevira to her family estates north of Londinium. They refused to accompany their father on the campaign against Ambrosius, or indeed to obey him at all.

A cheer rippled across the field, dragging Vortigern away from his bitter thoughts. One of his Saxons had stepped forward into the space between the opposing armies to offer a challenge to single combat.

"His name is Oisc, lord king," said Hengist, who stood at Vortigern's elbow, "a deadly fighter with the spear. One of Horsa's best men."

Vortigern watched Oisc stride confidently towards the lines of British infantry. He had stripped off his byrnie and undershirt, and was naked to the waist.

When he was within bow-shot of the enemy, he stopped, held up his spear and shield, and howled like a wolf. His cry met with another rousing cheer from the Saxons, and a chorus of jeers and insults from the Britons, but none of the latter stepped forward to accept his challenge.

"Cowards," Hengist said scornfully. Vortigern glanced sideways at him.

Hengist was scarcely recognisable as the ragged pirate who first presented himself at court, two summers gone. He wore a shining coat of mail almost as splendid as Vortigern's, and over it a cloak of dark blue wool lined with rabbit fur, clasped at the shoulder with an elaborate golden brooch. His dark brown hair and beard were immaculately groomed and powdered, and he had even been known tobathe. More gold ornaments, torcs and bangles, adorned his throat and wrists. The hilt of his sword was inlaid with precious stones, and the blade rested inside a wooden scabbard bound in leather and lined with sheep wool.

None of this splendour could outshine the gleam of Hengist's single eye, brimful of cold intelligence. Vortigern knew he had come to rely on the man too much, but feared the consequences if he tried to dismiss him.

Oisc howled again. Still there was no movement among the British ranks.

They hold their discipline. Ambrosius has drilled them well, damn him.

Ambrosius had arranged his infantry into four dense phalanxes of spearmen, with archers to the rear and bands of slingers and javelin-men guarding their flanks. Some eight hundred men, in all, with units of light cavalry on the wings.

Vortigern could see Ambrosius' dragon banner, fluttering to the rear of the British infantry. He wondered if they would meet, face-to-face in the thick of the fighting to come, and perish on each other's blades.

First, Ambrosius would have to carve his way through Vortigern's mercenaries. Six hundred Saxons, formed up into three divisions, the shields of the front ranks overlapping each other to form a wall.

Hengist's brother Horsa was in command of the central division. His giant figure could be easily picked out, standing under a V-shaped banner painted with the image of a wild boar. The Saxons regarded the beast as a symbol of strength and fertility, and the motif appeared everywhere: on their banners, engraved on their helmets, painted on their shields.

Vortigern's battered spirits lifted a little at the sight of his Saxons, the finest infantry seen in Britannia since the time of the legions. He had lavished much of his wealth and attention on them, and spared no expense on their war-gear.

"A magnificent sight, lord king," remarked Hengist, "my people will win your battle for you. Send them forward, and let us settle this affair."

Vortigern hesitated. Save for the futile howls of Oisc, a strange quiet had fallen over the field. It was a gaunt, cheerless day in late October, and in his mind's eye he glimpsed the pale shadow of death flitting across the scene.

This was the prelude, the hush before the killing started. It was almost peaceful, akin to the hallowed atmosphere inside the nave of a church.

Hengist shifted impatiently. "Order the attack, lord king," he said in a tone bordering on arrogance, as though the High King was his servant.

Still Vortigern said nothing. He wanted the peace to last forever. All he had ever wanted was a peaceful, prosperous land. Instead he had led his people to this killing ground.

Now they stood ranged against him, while he was forced to rely on sell-swords. Vortigern bowed his head in shame. Perhaps it would be better to turn, slink back to Londinium, and resign his title.

Then Oisc howled again.

*

AMBROSIUS

"Put me in an arrow in that fool's throat," Ambrosius ordered, "a solidus to the man who shuts his noise."

Five of his archers took up the challenge, and bent their bows. They stood on slightly rising ground, ten feet or so behind the infantry, and the wind was in their favour.

Ambrosius watched as five arrows sailed into the bone-white skies, marked here and there with smudges of grey cloud.

Four missed, if narrowly, thudding into the hard ground either side of the Saxon champion's feet. The fifth shot true, and skewered his gullet.

The strange hush was broken by a storm of shouts and cheers, torn from British throats as the Saxon's spear slowly fell from his stiffening fingers. Their voices rose to a crescendo as he dropped dead to the ground.

Ambrosius dug in the pouch at his belt. "Fine shot," he said, grinning at the archer who had loosed the fateful arrow, and flipped the silver coin at him.

The archer caught it in his left hand and swiftly pocketed it. Money of any kind was becoming increasingly rare. A silver solidus would buy enough wine to keep him drunk for a week.

If he lives, thought Ambrosius, *if any of us do.*

Enraged at the dishonourable killing of their champion, the Saxons were responding to the British cheers with curses and insults, clashing their weapons against their shields, working themselves up into a frenzy.

The sight of their battle-array was enough to make any man tremble. Ambrosius nervously ran his tongue over his lips, and glanced right and left to check the dispositions of his army for the hundredth time. A thousand men, almost the full strength of the comitatenses, bar a few auxiliaries he left behind to garrison the forts.

When news of Vortigern's advance from Londinium had reached him, Ambrosius immediately marched from Mons Ambrius to block the highway leading from the capital to Sorviodunum, another ancient hill-fort once occupied by the Romans, and the heart of the fertile region he sought to defend.

He had chosen to make a stand here, on the eastern fringe of a wide river valley. Nearby lay a village called Guoloph. The rear of his army was guarded by dense woodland, with patches of low-lying marshy ground and scrubby trees affording some protection to its flanks.

Vortigern's banners appeared just after noon, heralded by the deep-throated singing of his Saxons. The High King's mercenaries were supported by a few native levies, supplied by the handful of British nobles who remained loyal to him.

Ambrosius kept forty of his cavalry in reserve and divided the rest into two wings of eighty men, commanded by the dependable veterans Gwri and Menas. The cavalry stood on the flanks of his battle-line, formed up into wedges, their banners fluttering in the gentle breeze.

His plan was simple. The British infantry would hold their ground, enticing the Saxons into committing all their forces to a frontal assault. Once they were engaged, the cavalry would swoop round the edges of the field and charge the enemy, flank and rear. Attacked from all sides at once, the Saxon shieldwall would crumble.

Gwri had suggested this strategy during a council of war at Mons Ambrius. Sketched out on a sheet of vellum with a piece of charcoal, it had looked neat and logical. Now Ambrosius was confronted with the reality of the Saxon host, flesh and blood in place of little squares and triangles on a map, it all seemed very different.

His blood froze as the thunderous drone of bull-horns rose from the Saxon lines, and the shieldwall started to tramp forward. They were coming.

"Archers!" Ambrosius shouted. His bowmen stooped to pluck arrows from the sheaves stuck into the ground at their feet.

"Notch-draw-loose!" cried their officers. A hail of arrows briefly darkened the sky.

They dropped into the front ranks of the Saxons, who flung their shields up to protect their faces. Most of the arrows stuck harmlessly into the hide coverings, but here and there a man dropped, stepped over or trampled on by his comrades.

AMBROSIUS

Ambrosius' heart beat like a drum as he watched his infantry brace for what was about to hit them. This was what they had drilled so many countless hours for on the plains outside Mons Ambrius.

"Lads, remember the words of that old sot, the Emperor Tiberius," he recalled Menas saying to the troops, "let our drills be like bloody battles, and our battles be like bloody drills!"

Roman-style discipline might be falling away among the British, but their tactics in battle were not entirely forgotten. As the Saxons came within throwing distance, the front three ranks of the British squares parted slightly, and the soldiers drew back their javelins.

The javelins were called veruta, short throwing missiles with tapering iron heads. Ambrosius' fingers tightened on his reins as the order to cast swept down the line, and a second lethal rain flew into the densely-packed Saxon ranks.

Unlike the arrows, the veruta did real damage, and Ambrosius' lips curled into a snarl as he saw many Saxons go down under the hail of iron-tipped darts. Hope surged inside him as he thought the shieldwall was breaking up, but fresh warriors rushed forward to plug the gaps opened by their fallen comrades.

His eyes fixed upon one especially huge Saxon chieftain standing under a V-shaped banner, roaring his men on like a maddened bull. This mountain of flesh and mail could only be Horsa. Ambrosius had never set eyes on him before, but he lived up to the rumours of his colossal strength and size.

The British lines closed up again as the re-formed shieldwall rumbled forward, and then the two hosts met with a shuddering crash and a splintering of shields and spears that reverberated across the field and inside Ambrosius' body.

"Hold," he muttered under his breath, "hold them. Stand firm – stand firm, for God's sake!"

The British infantry outnumbered the Saxons, but they were less well-armed, and none save the officers wore mail. Few had ever seen action beyond the training field, while the men they faced were all seasoned warriors. They met the grinding weight and power of the Saxon assault with all the courage and discipline they could muster, but it wasn't enough.

Saxon long-axes carved through the British lines, cleaving men apart like old parchment, wetting the trampled grass with blood and brains and steaming entrails. Horsa's division ploughed forward with unstoppable force, mowing down the British spearmen in their path, shattering their formation like a mailed fist punching through a spider's web. Horsa himself performed savage wonders of war, laughing and singing as he laid about him with his blood-soaked axe, chopping down every brave man who dared to oppose him.

Panic rose in Ambrosius' throat. In desperation he looked to his cavalry, but Menas and Gwri knew their trade.

The British horsemen surged forward, the screams of their bugles tearing through the din of battle. As planned, they galloped around the edges of the fighting and hurled their javelins into the tight-packed Saxon ranks.

Ambrosius cantered forward to meet the stream of fugitives fleeing from Horsa's savage assault.

"Stand firm, you spineless women," he cried, striking at them with the flat of his sword, "where will you run to? Who will defend your homes and families? There can be no retreat from here – it is victory or death! Turn, turn and fight!" A few were shamed into obeying, though many more ignored him and vanished into the woods, dropping their weapons as they ran. Those who stayed hastily formed some apology for a battle-line, their feeble ranks bolstered by the skirmishers Ambrosius ordered to join them.

"Fight," he yelled, his voice growing hoarse with shouting, "fight for your lives, for all you hold dear. Strike down these base robbers and pirates, these filthy pagan idolaters, and assure your place in Heaven. Fight, and be comforted. God is in every blow!"

*

"I will send in the reserve," said Vortigern, "and lead them myself."

He straightened his back. Something like vigour coursed through him. The time for decisive action had come, to put his own body in the way of danger, and the crushing weight of dread instantly lifted from his shoulders.

He had watched the battle unfold in silence, struggling against the conflicting storms that raged inside him. The slaughter of the British infantry filled him with a baffling mixture of hope and sorrow, and he didn't know whether to weep or cheer when Ambrosius' cavalry rescued the situation, storming around the fringes of the battlefield to cave in the flanks of the Saxon shieldwall.

The fighting had reached a bloody, futile stalemate, neither side willing to yield a foot of ground. Unless he acted, Vortigern could see no victory for anyone here.

He looked proudly at his bodyguard. Their moment had come. They would follow their lord into battle, and win glory or death. Perhaps both: Vortigern no longer placed much value on his own life, and suddenly relished the thought of meeting a warrior's end, sword in hand.

Hengist seized his bridle.

"No, lord king," he said softly, "throw in your reserves if you will, but you cannot lead them. What if you fell in battle? How should we cope without our High King? Would you make my sweet sister a widow?"

Hengist's single eye possessed an almost hypnotic quality. Its steely grey light thrust like a sword, deep into Vortigern's soul, slicing easily through the crusted layers of bluster and deceit.

To his shame, he yielded. "Very well," he muttered, "Guechta can lead them instead."

Hengist signalled to his kinsman, who trotted over from his place at the head of Vortigern's personal guard. The two briefly spoke in their own tongue, and then Guechta wheeled his horse and rode back to his command.

They learn quickly, Vortigern thought. When he first came to Britannia, Guechta had never backed a horse in his life. Now he rode, if not superbly, at least well enough to lead cavalry in battle.

The trumpet sounded, and his buccelari galloped into the fray, led by the bulky figure of their Saxon officer. In their wake charged the small detachments of native infantry Vortigern had brought to the field, spearmen and slingers and a handful of archers, to add their weight to the attack.

Vortigern was left with just Hengist and a few attendants for company. His personal standard, displaying a golden eagle with outspread wings woven against a red field, rippled overhead.

He watched his people slaughter each other under a steadily darkening sky. Rain started to fall. The battle disintegrated, collapsing into hundreds of isolated melees and single combats. Vortigern's reinforcements had only added more bodies to the dreadful press, and did little to swing the tide in his favour.

The world was blood. Nothing but blood, smearing the flanks of the valley, painting the green grass a livid shade of red. The soldiers of both sides were mingled together, a hopelessly confused mob of angry and frightened men hacking and clawing at each other, all order dissolved, banners waving uselessly, officers losing touch with their commands.

Those on the edges of the chaos started to creep away, into the safety of the woods and marshes. Vortigern saw plenty of his own men among the deserters, but lacked the will to call them back.

After two hours of vicious fighting, the contending armies had virtually ceased to exist. The battle spilled into the woods, and the rain brought with it heavy mist, rising from the nearby river to drape the scene of slaughter in cloying grey folds.

"We should depart," Vortigern said in a hollow voice, "there is nothing to be gained here."

Hengist looked pale and strained, his single eye narrowed to a slit as it searched the misted, blood-tainted field. Men emerged and vanished again in the murk, maimed and bleeding from terrible wounds. There was no sign of Horsa, last seen in the thickest of the fight, still laying about him with his axe.

"Do as you will, lord king," he replied, "I will not quit the field without my brother."

AMBROSIUS

No victory here, Vortigern thought despairingly, *nothing but a feast of death, a banquet for the wolves and ravens that will come creeping from the woods once the bloody day is done.*

There was nothing for it but to turn and withdraw east, back to his safe haven in Londinium. There Vortigern might rebuild his shattered fortunes, and try to forge a new army from the survivors who managed to crawl back to the city.

With a heavy heart, he slowly turned his horse and rode east, towards the highway. His attendants followed.

Vortigern glanced back, once, at Hengist. The Saxon made for a lonely figure, raindrops bouncing off his helmet and soaking through his fine cloak. He stood like a statue, waiting for his brother.

He would wait, Vortigern knew, until the breaking of the world.

"May the Devil take them both," the High King muttered, and urged his horse into a canter.

*

Dusk fell, mercifully shrouding the field of pain and death. Some figures still staggered to and fro, more like ghosts than men, wandering aimlessly among the heaps of human wreckage.

Occasionally, rising above the piteous moans of the wounded and dying, there could be heard the weary clash of steel. The futile conflict was not quite done. A few of the living still fought, attempting to butcher each other with mindless savagery.

Ambrosius raised his broken javelin, plucked from a twitching corpse, to ward off a sword-thrust. His arms were sluggish, heavy as lead, the muscles and sinews aching with stress and exhaustion. Blood flowed turgidly from a gash on the bicep of his right shoulder.

His Saxon opponent was even slower, and the sword thudded dully against the iron shaft of the javelin. The Saxon hissed through his broken teeth and collapsed to his knees. He was slathered from head to toe in mud, his byrnie hanging him off like an ill-fitting cloak, torn and pierced in many places.

Ambrosius drew back his javelin for the killing blow, but there was no need. The Saxon had dropped his sword and doubled over, still hissing, clutching at a tear in his side. Dark red blood flowed over his filthy fingers. He had taken a wound earlier in the fighting, and his last thrust had torn something in his vitals.

It seemed a kindness to kill him, so Ambrosius left the man to die slowly. He was himself faint and light-headed with loss of blood, and scarcely knew where he was going as he limped away, towards the greater darkness of the forest.

He tripped over the foreleg of a dead horse and fell on his hands and knees in the wet mud. For a few seconds he stayed there, trying not to gag at the raw, all-pervading stench of battle: congealing blood, sweat and terror and spilled entrails, split guts, urine and excrement, death and horror and despair.

A black shape fluttered down to perch on the mangled belly of a dead British infantryman, lying sprawled on his back just a foot or so from Ambrosius, the dead man staring at the living with glassy, unseeing eyes.

His stomach was cut open, probably by a Saxon axe. Blood oozed from the ragged hole. The raven cocked its head at Ambrosius, decided he wasn't worth the effort, and started to peck at the corpse's eyeballs.

"Christ save me," mumbled Ambrosius. His legs shook as he tried to stand, and he had to use the javelin as a crutch.

He was alive – alive, when so many of his soldiers were not. God had spared him, almost certainly as a punishment.

There were more dead horses scattered about here, on the verge of the woods, animal shapes lying next to their riders. The red cloaks of Ambrosius' men contrasted with the blue of Vortigern's. A straight fight between opposing cavalry, ending in roughly equal numbers of slain.

Ambrosius had lost count of the number of skirmishes, charges and counter-charges. The details of the battle were a meaningless jumble in his shattered mind.

Men fought. Men died, or fled. That is the truth of it.

He lurched into the woods. His horse was dead, her throat slashed by a Saxon blade. His helmet was gone, a battered, dented and useless object, lying somewhere among all the rest of the broken and abandoned war-gear scattered over the field. His sword and shield were gone. Ambrosius had a vague memory of his blade lodging in a Saxon's ribs, and snapping off when he tried to wrench it out. God knew what had become of his shield.

His army was gone. Both sides had destroyed each other in the valley of Guoloph, all the years of careful planning and recruitment brought to ruin in a single afternoon.

Breathing heavily, Ambrosius leaned against a tree. Random, fractured images of the past few hours stumbled through his memory.

Menas and Gwri were dead. He had seen them die, clawed from their saddles in the heat of the press, held down and hacked to pieces by the murderous long-axes. Both whimpered and fouled themselves before they died. A bad end, for such loyal and able comrades.

What was a good end, in battle? To die like a warrior - like a man, as his father might say - sword in hand and facing the enemy, was to die like a pig gone for slaughter, squealing in terror and agony, bowels squirting as the blades bit deep.

Horsa was also dead, or at least Ambrosius thought he was. The gigantic Saxon warrior had suffered hideous injuries, enough to fell any lesser man. Ambrosius himself had thrust a javelin into him, to join the five others protruding from his massive back.

Bleeding and bellowing, his huge body a mass of open wounds, Horsa had seemed invulnerable, until a cavalryman galloped in from behind and impaled him with a spear. Ambrosius last saw him lying on his side, trying to pull the shaft out of his stomach, while his loyal gesiths closed around their chief, chanting death-songs.

Ambrosius blinked and shook his head, willing away the memories. There was no time to indulge them now, or dwell on the horrors of battle. He had to live, to return to his headquarters at Mons Ambrius, and rally what was left of the comitatenses.

At least Vortigern had been checked. He could not take the harvested grain now, which would lie safely inside the barns and storehouses of the network of forts to the west.

Nor, Ambrosius reflected, did he have such pressing need of it. At Guoloph, the number of Saxon mouths Vortigern was required to feed had been drastically reduced.

The High King would come again, though, and Ambrosius would have to be ready for him.

Leaning heavily on his makeshift crutch, he forced himself to take one step, then another, and another, until the shadows of the forest had swallowed him up.

The dead on the field were left to the beasts and birds of the forest, a fit meal for such carrion-eaters:

"Let them dispose of the corpses,
Enjoy the foods,
The greedy war-hawk,
The dusky raven,
And that grey shadow,
The wolf in the wood."

12.

Sevira, daughter of Magnus Maximus and ex-consort to the High King, yawned and rubbed her tired eyes.

If matters had turned out differently, Sevira reflected as she stared gloomily at the abysmal handwriting of her steward, *I might have been an Empress – or, at the very least, married off to some enormously rich and influential Roman senator.*

She allowed herself to daydream for a moment. The alternative Sevira would have resided in unimaginable luxury in the great palaces of Rome or Constantinople, surrounded by an army of slaves and handsome young men.

This glorious destiny was thwarted when her father's well of good fortune ran dry in Dalmatia. After his death, Sevira and her sister were raised by their widowed mother on the family estates north of Londinium. Her sister had died young of a mysterious stomach illness, leaving Sevira the sole heir to their father's possessions.

She now sat at her mother's writing desk in the Scriptorium, poring over the estate accounts for the previous month.

It made for depressing as well as dull reading. Her family estates may have been large, almost four thousand acres divided into five sizeable villas, but they were slowly decaying. There simply weren't enough slaves and freemen left to farm the land adequately, or overseers to manage them.

My lands, thought Sevira, *are the Western Empire in miniature. Ragged at the edges, and steadily dwindling to nothing.*

She read through the wage bills with a growing sense of despair and unease. Since the collapse of the Roman economy in Gaul, and the virtual cease of trade between Britannia and the Continent, money had become an increasingly rare commodity.

Some of the richer British nobles and landowners had taken to hoarding money, as though deliberately keeping the stuff out of circulation would help matters. With money, even the concept of money, increasingly devalued, the country was sliding back to the barter system of ancient pre-Roman days, with services paid for in goods instead of coin.

In effect, this meant Sevira was forced to pay her servants and freemen in clothing and foodstuffs, or even livestock. As a proud descendent of Roman aristocracy, Sevira despised this barbaric practice, but was obliged to follow it. Her own private store of silver pennies was savagely depleted, and now consisted of less then eighty solidi kept inside a locked chest under her bed.

"What are we becoming?" she said aloud, leaning her elbows on the desk, "what can redeem us?"

As if on cue, she overheard men's voices outside, and the thump of wooden swords.

Bored and irritated with paperwork, she stood up and crossed to the window. It was square in shape, with a wooden frame and square panes of tinted blue glass in the lattice.

Glass was also an increasingly rare luxury. Only the very wealthiest could still obtain it, and Sevira wished to project the illusion of wealth for as long as possible. Wealth meant power, and power equalled security.

As the unpopular ex-wife of the High King, she had a great need for security. Sevira lived in fear of knives and poisons, or soldiers suddenly appearing at the gate with orders to arrest her. The Saxon whore, Rowena – she grimaced at the mere thought of her rival's name – would not rest until Sevira was lying cold in the ground.

Sevira had little cause to smile these days, but the corners of her mouth twitched as she peered through the glass. The Scriptorium overlooked the gardens and a cobbled forecourt, and she could see two men sparring on a neatly trimmed square of lawn beside a statue of Venus.

The statue was a trophy brought back by her father from the wars in North Africa, where he had helped Count Theodosius to suppress a rebellion. Sevira dimly recalled sitting at her mother's knee as a child, thrilling to the stories of Magnus' military exploits.

AMBROSIUS

Poor woman, Sevira thought sadly, *she loved him, and he left her to follow a fool's dream. She was left with nothing but stories to comfort her, and two whining little girls.*

Her mother had at least lived long enough to see the birth of her first grandchild, Vortimer. All through the pregnancy, Sevira prayed for a son, and God granted her wish.

Two more boys followed. Strong, healthy boys, who made Vortigern's palace at Viroconium both hideous and wonderful with their noise.

Her second son, Catigern, was one of the men sparring on the lawn. He and his opponent, a greying ex-soldier Sevira employed as a trainer in weapons and horsemanship, vigorously hacked and stabbed at each other with wooden spathas. They carried light practice shields, and wore no armour save helmets.

Sevira rapped her knuckles on the window pane. "Can't you see it's raining, you fools?" she cried, "you will catch a chill!"

They didn't hear her, or pretended not to. In common with his brothers, Catigern was fiercely competitive, and spent every spare moment trying to improve his mind and body. Since infancy, they had strived to outdo each other, and fought like wildcats.

She frowned. Catigern was fighting in earnest, even though it was meant to be a practice bout, pressing his opponent hard and driving him back with savage ferocity. He was taking an unfair advantage. The trainer, Gallus, could hardly respond in kind. He was permitted to mark Catigern, but faced flogging or dismissal if he hurt him too badly.

"That is his father's gift," murmured Sevira, resting her fingers on the glass. She had nurtured her sons, done her best to ensure they grew up into fine, upstanding men, fitting grandsons of Maximus, but it was impossible to completely rub out the taint of Vortigern's blood.

Her eldest son, Vortimer, was out hunting in the deep forest bordering the western edge of the estate. He had a passion for hunting, and would return at dusk, tired but happy, with several fat does, maybe even a boar, carried on poles by his slaves.

Sevira had the boys all to herself, ever since they broke with their father. She knew the sundering of the family had caused them much distress, almost as much as it caused her. Only her youngest, Pascent, had remained at court with Vortigern, albeit more out of duty than love.

By now Catigern had succeeded in beating Gallus to his knees, and was holding the edge of his spatha against the other man's throat. Gallus yielded, and Catigern turned to hold up his sword and shield in triumph, his ruddily handsome features flushed with victory. Rain soaked through the thin wool of his tunic, outlining the severe contours of his hard, muscular body, and flattened his curling brown hair against his skull.

He was gazing up at the window of the Scriptorium, clearly aware of his mother's eyes upon him.

"Still a child," said Sevira, smiling and fluttering her fingers at him, "desperate for my approval. Will my boys ever grow up?"

Later, she would quietly apologise to Gallus, maybe even compensate him. The man was loyal, and had been in the service of her family for years. Equally, when Catigern's blood had cooled a little, she would admonish him for taking advantage of a faithful servant. Such people should be treasured, not abused. There were few enough of them to be found in these degraded latter days.

Her eyes felt a little better. With deep reluctance, but compelled by the overriding sense of duty that defined her life, Sevira returned to her desk.

They came for her that evening. Vortimer had returned, and was boasting to his family over supper of his hunting exploits, when an elderly slave named Totia hurried into the triclinium.

"My apologies, mistress," he said, ducking his white head in Sevira's direction, "but a troop of riders are fast approaching from the south road. Thirty men, under the eagle banner."

Sevira sat bolt upright on her couch. The south road was the main route to Londinium.

Vortimer and Catigern were already on their feet, calling for their armour.

"No," she cried, even as more slaves hurried in with their sword-belts, "there will be no bloodshed. Whatever my husband's soldiers want with me, we shall not give them an excuse for violence. Am I understood?" His sons were grown men, but still quailed under the lash of their mother's voice.

"We can't let them take you without a fight," Vortimer said sullenly, "nor would you expect us to."

"They may not want to take me at all," replied Sevira, forcing a note of confidence into her voice, "Totia, go to the gate. If these men demand entry, let them in. We shall await them here."

Sevira knew it was vital to keep her composure, if only for appearance's sake. If Vortigern had indeed sent men to arrest or even kill her, she would not have it said that she failed to meet her fate with dignity.

What of her sons? Her only real fear was for them, but not even Vortigern would order the killing of his own children.

Unless his Saxon whore has promised him more and better sons....

Sevira quelled her doubts. She had her friends in Londinium, and would have known if Rowena was with child. With luck, the bitch would prove barren, and Vortigern would cast her aside with the same cold, uncaring ruthlessness he had shown his first wife.

In spite of her wishes, Vortimer and Catigern had buckled on their swords, and stood protectively before their mother while shouts and marching footsteps echoed in the passage outside.

Totia had closed the double doors behind him, but now they were flung open by two hard-faced burly soldiers in long mail shirts and cavalry helmets. Ten more filed in behind them and spread out in two lines either side of the doorway.

Their officer was last. Sevira, who had held herself perfectly still and upright as the soldiers marched in, almost buckled with relief when she saw him.

The officer was Pascent, her youngest son. A little older and thinner than the last time she saw him, over six months gone, but still her child.

Of all her boys, Pascent physically resembled their father the most: stocky and below medium height, plain of face and with muddy brown hair and a dark complexion. His brothers had inherited their famous grandsire's height and graceful build, but Pascent was unremarkable to look at.

For all that, he was also the most practical and dutiful of them, and had learned the art of compromise.

He halted in the doorway, took off his helmet and raised his right hand in an old-fashioned Roman salute.

"I'm sorry to invade you like this," he said, beaming amiably at his kin, "but father insisted. I would have been happy to come with just a few servants for company."

"Still running errands for him, traitor?" spat Catigern, who had never forgiven his sibling for staying true to Vortigern.

Pascent ignored the jibe. "Brothers," he said, "I must ask you to hand over your swords. They make my men nervous."

Vortimer and Catigern instantly fell into a fighting stance, hands clapped to their sword-hilts. "Those Saxon pigs behind you may rip our swords from our dead fingers," Vortimer hissed through his teeth, "but not before."

Sevira broke the tension by clapping her hands. "Enough of this play-acting," she cried, stepping between her sons, "Pascent, I have not seen you for over half a year, but prefer not to believe you have turned into a kinslayer during that time. If your brothers give up their weapons, do you swear not to harm them?"

Pascent's mild brown eyes had a faintly bruised expression. "Are things grown so bad between us," he said sadly, "that I must swear an oath not to murder you all out of hand?"

He got no answer, and so heaved a heavy sigh and raised his right hand. "I swear, on my honour as a soldier, on my fidelity as a son, and on my faith as a Christian, not to harm a precious hair on the precious heads of either of my precious brothers. There. Does that satisfy you?"

"It will have to," said Sevira, and turned to her other sons. "Give up your swords, you boneheads, and hand them over."

Vortimer and Catigern hesitated, but neither could endure their mother's stare for long. Somewhat sheepishly, they drew their swords and held them out, hilt-first, to Pascent's soldiers.

"Now, then," Sevira added when the tension had relaxed a little, "do I never get a hug from my youngest child?"

Pascent's answering smile was warm, and so was his embrace. Having done her best to ease the situation, Sevira went so far as to wink at him and pinch his cheek.

To her delight, he still coloured easily. "Listen, all of you," he said, coughing to hide his embarrassment, "much as I would wish it, I am not here to exchange pleasantries. Father...the High King sent me here for a reason."

"You snake," rasped Catigern, starting forward, "you mean to arrest us after all!"

A few of Pascent's Saxons reached for their blades, but he gestured at them to stand down.

"Please, Catigern," he said reasonably, "I didn't expect you to fall weeping on my neck, but let us at least be civil to each other. The High King did not send me to arrest you, though he anticipated some resistance, hence the presence of all these armed villains behind me."

"The truth is, he wants you back at court. The king needs all his sons. We are the only people he can trust. Those were his very words, which he asked me to convey."

Vortimer snorted with mirthless laughter. "What of Hengist?" he demanded, "has our father tired of being the Saxon's plaything?"

Pascent turned and signalled at his men to leave. They marched out with the same orderly precision with which they had entered, and he pushed the doors shut after them.

"Now," he said with another of his gentle smiles, "we can have some privacy. Some of my men are Hengist's kin – they breed like vermin, those folk – and would not bear to hear ill spoken of him."

"Hengist's influence grows by the day, and the king is both weary and frightened of him. Those councillors who remain loyal to us will no longer come to Londinium. The city is stuffed full of Saxon troops and their families."

"So father wants us to come and help redress the balance, does he?" sneered Vortimer, "I will not see him again. Not until he renounces his whore and makes a public apology to our mother, in the presence of all the assembled nobles and churchmen of the land."

"Even then," added Catigern, refusing to be outdone, "I will not set foot within a mile of Londinium until every last Saxon is ejected, and Hengist and his brother hanged from the city walls."

Pascent looked at them hopelessly. "Brothers," he said, throwing up his hands, "you cannot expect me to take such an answer back to the king. He would be forced to declare you both traitors, and have you imprisoned. How long do you think you would survive then, with Hengist whispering poison into his ear?"

Sevira had listened to the exchange carefully, her mind churning. It seemed Vortigern had finally realised the consequences of his folly, and was desperate to free himself from the insidious influence of Hengist and Horsa.

She thought rapidly. In the three years since the mutual disaster of Guoloph, Vortigern and his enemies had dug in and concentrated on rebuilding their military strength. Britannia was turning into an armed camp, with two factions glowering at each other over a boundary line running roughly through the middle of the country. There was little actual fighting, since both sides were wary of risking another pitched battle, but war had only been delayed, not averted.

With few allies left among his countrymen, Vortigern was forced to rely on a steady flow of Saxon mercenaries coming over the North Sea. Meantime his principal enemy, Ambrosius, was busily throwing up a huge series of linear earthworks to protect his headquarters in the west.

Sevira had never met or even seen Ambrosius. Had Vortigern not set her aside, she felt confident she could have brought them both to the negotiating table. The conflict between them was sheer folly, and bled the country of men and resources.

All the while, Britannia's coasts continued to suffer from raids, and the Picts and the Scotti slowly recovered from their stinging defeat at Deva.

She was loath to admit it, but perhaps this effort at reconciliation was a step towards peace. "What of me?" she asked, "did your father have any message for his ex-wife?"

Pascent hung his head. "No, mother. He made no mention of you."

It was a calculated insult. Vortigern always knew how to hurt her. Twenty years of marriage, sharing in his victories and defeats, bearing his children, had come to this.

"We need not detain you, my son," she said brightly, "you heard your brothers. There can be no reconciliation with the High King, unless he sets aside Hengist's sister and makes a public apology to me."

The more grovelling the better, she added silently, *and even then it won't be enough. I shall make him crawl like a worm before the eyes of the world.*

Pascent looked crestfallen, so she clasped his hand. "Once your father has made his penance," she said, "he can have the rest of his sons back. Until then, never."

13.

The great lump of volcanic rock rose from the surrounding landscape like the curving back of a whale. Lights glimmered near the top, throwing into silhouette the long line of wooden towers and turf ramparts that ran the entire length of the crest.

It was evening, and God had granted Ambrosius an impossibly beautiful view. The sun hung low in the sky, casting waves of crimson light over the rock, the bottom half of which was wreathed in mist. If he narrowed his eyes, it almost seemed to hover above the land, stranded between myth and reality.

Ambrosius had never seen anything like it. Compared to this, Mons Ambrius was a mere doll's house perched on a molehill.

The town built on top of the mighty rock was called Curia, and the home of a British tribe called the Votadini. It had taken Ambrosius the best part of a month to journey here, riding north along the old Roman highways to Eburucum, capital of Britannia Secunda, and then venturing beyond the Wall.

He had never been so far north – never even seen the Wall until the Council despatched him on this mission. At first he had resented being sent up here, like some glorified envoy, but now felt grateful for the respite from war and politics.

The wild north country had stirred something deep in his soul. Riding through the beautiful desolation of the dales, deserted save for sheep and a few scattered hill-farms, was like escaping to another world. He briefly allowed himself the luxury of imagining he might never return.

Harsh reality intruded when he beheld the city of Eburucum, situated at the confluence of two rivers. Once the capital of Britannia Inferior, one of the four subdivided Roman provinces of Britannia, it was now the heart of the semi-independent lordship of Ebrauc, ruled by a warlord named Coel Hen, or Coel the Old.

Ambrosius had been warned about Coel. Wily and utterly ruthless, he had stamped his authority all over a significant chunk of the north, from Eburucum to a large stretch of territory beyond the Wall. The petty chiefs and lesser tribes all acknowledged his superiority, and owed fealty to him rather than the High King in Londinium. In turn, and to avoid any interference in his affairs from the south, he paid annual tribute to Vortigern, usually in the form of arms and livestock.

Eburucum was surrounded with stone walls. They were in a poor state of repair, mended in places with piles of timber and earth, but spears glinted on the walkway above the southern gate, and Coel's banners flew from the turrets. They displayed a stag with spreading antlers, worked in yellow thread against an emerald green field.

"Enter, friend," said one of the sentries when Ambrosius had made himself known, "but you may only bring five men inside the city with you."

Ambrosius had come north with a sizeable escort, eighty of his father's buccelari. They had clearly impressed the men on the gate, and made them nervous of his intentions.

Not wishing to cause offence or raise suspicion, Ambrosius consented, and ordered the majority of his command to pitch camp outside the walls. The gates creaked inwards, and he trotted inside with just five men at his back.

"I have come from Londinium," he informed the sentry who came down to greet him, "on a mission from the Council of Britannia. An envoy was sent to your master. He should be expecting me."

The sentry bowed. "Follow me, lord," he said, "I shall take you to the king."

King, thought Ambrosius, *King of Eburucum, and Lord of the North. This warlord does not hesitate to give himself airs.*

He took careful note of the city. Like so many Roman settlements, it had declined sharply in recent years, but Coel had made some effort to repair the crumbling fortifications and re-occupy the deserted residential quarter.

Sadly, his workmen lacked the craft to restore the glories of old. As Ambrosius rode through the streets, guiding his horse around piles of rubbish, he noted the dilapidated state of the shops and houses. Maybe one in three was occupied, and had

111

fresh plaster on the walls. The others were boarded up, home to nothing save rats and pigeons.

At least the defences were in good order. The ditches outside the walls had been re-dug and widened, and a new tower constructed on the outer wall.

Coel Hen had turned the old Roman fortress in the centre of the city into a palace. Built on the north bank of one of the rivers, it was a self-contained town in itself, guarded by a five-metre high wall of stone. Ambrosius saw two huge angular towers, twice the size of the wall and projecting from the western and southern corners, with six smaller towers at intervals between them. These defences were formidable, allowing the defenders to shoot down and through the sides of the wall.

He and his escort were admitted through the gate facing the river, and led through the neat grid of streets and barracks to the sprawling complex of Coel's palace in the centre. In stark contrast to the rotting, half-deserted city outside, the streets were in good repair and bustling with people, warriors and clerks rubbing shoulders with slaves, labourers and tradesmen. The southern corner of the fort was taken up by a huge bath-house, pillared and colonnaded, and elsewhere Ambrosius saw barracks, workshops, granaries, even a hospital.

The palace was a huge structure, almost as grand as the one in Londinium. Built around a central courtyard, it was dominated by a great aisled basilica, over twenty metres in height. A range of lesser buildings adjoined the basilica, including a large two-storey house with a tiled and gabled roof, which Ambrosius assumed to be the old praetorium. Once a private residence for the Roman officer in charge of the garrison, it would now serve as home to Coel, his family and slaves.

Coel himself proved to be a splendid old tyrant. He met Ambrosius inside the roofed section of the basilica, a long, rectangular chamber with red and black tiles on the floor, divided in two by a row of arched pillars.

The Lord of the North was a stout, bearish man with a carefully groomed mane of white hair flowing to his shoulders, and a forked beard. He wore a robe of a startling bright yellow colour, made of some rich fabric Ambrosius didn't recognise.

"Silk, all the way from Constantinople," grinned Coel, showing thick yellow teeth to match his robe, "trade may have fallen away in recent times, but we still get a precious item or two, brought by traders from overseas."

And more besides, Ambrosius was willing to wager. Coel clearly did very well for himself. The hilt of his sword was spectacular. Its pommel was inlaid with gold and garnet fittings, the guards plated with gold, and the grip bore two gold mounts decorated with delicate silver filigree.

No-one else, not even Vortigern, owned so fine a sword. Ambrosius smiled wryly as he recalled the last annual tribute from Eburucum had consisted of eleven underfed cows, three of them lame, and a single wagonload of inferior armour and weapons, all red with rust.

He spent just one night in the king's rough company. Coel talked little of business and much of himself, the glory of his achievements, the bloody slaughters he had inflicted on his enemies. He was tedious and overbearing, but Ambrosius managed to slip in a few questions about the state of the Wall's defences.

"Whatever else you may call yourself, you are also the governor of Eburucum," he said, "and responsible for the Wall's upkeep."

Coel looked evasive, his little blue eyes flickering like flies trapped in a jar.

"Most of the main forts are garrisoned," he replied brusquely, "though I am hard-put to find enough men. The damned Wall is eighty miles long! Vortigern cannot expect me to man every single tower and outpost."

"Where do you get the men?" asked Ambrosius.

The old ruffian gulped down another goblet of wine, his seventh of the night, before answering.

"Set thieves to catch thieves," he replied, spreading his mouth in another toothy grin, and refused to say any more on the matter.

They talked awhile of Ambrosius' mission, and the state of affairs in the south, until Coel started yawning. He was very drunk by now, and had to be carried to his bedchamber by four hefty slaves. Ambrosius was left alone to brood in the small triclinium behind the basilica, where Coel entertained important visitors.

When he wanted to sleep, another of Coel's slaves escorted him to a bedchamber, while his men were given beds in one of the barrack-houses outside the palace.

A whore was waiting for him. She was about fifteen years old, pale-skinned and red-haired, and naked as a needle under the covers.

"I am a gift," she announced, as the slave departed with a smirk, "from the Lord of the North. He bids you use me as you will."

She was pretty, in a freckled, snub-nosed sort of way, and the fragrant odour of her rose-scented perfume filled the room. Ambrosius swallowed as she peeled back the blanket to reveal her pale nakedness.

"Out," he said, looking anywhere but at her, "I am a married man."

"And I am a married woman," she laughed, "though I have lost count of my husbands."

"Out!"

Shrugging, she swung her long legs out of bed, stretched languorously, and picked up her gown from the chair beside the bed.

She slipped on the gown and walked slowly past him, swaying her hips slightly. Her elbow brushed his. Ambrosius looked away, reddening, and strived to ignore the torch-lit armies of lust marching through his vitals.

He spent a restless night, cursing his host and praying desperately for the cool balm of sleep.

It failed to come. Ambrosius was up before first light, exhausted and light-headed, and made his way to the barracks to collect his men.

AMBROSIUS

The dawn sun was a mere edge of light, glimmering over the horizon to the east, when he rode out of Eburucum and turned north.

14.

"Set thieves to catch thieves."

Ambrosius puzzled over these words until he reached Vercovicium, an auxiliary fort located on a stretch of the Wall some fifty miles north-west of Eburucum.

The state of the fort was both depressing and frightening. The walls were crumbling and collapsed in places, worn away by decades of neglect and appalling weather, and the men looked like they would flee at the first sign of a Pict. Either that, or join forces with them in pillaging the country.

Only now did Coel's words reveal their meaning. The quality of the garrison mirrored their surroundings. Even the foederati of the Saxon Shore made a better show than these slovenly, villainous-looking characters, more like brigands and cattle thieves than soldiers. There was barely enough of them to occupy half the fort, a compact rectangular enclosure guarded by stone walls and towers.

Ambrosius realised what was happening. Lacking enough warriors to defend the Wall, Coel was manning the forts with criminals. Mere gallows-bait, good for hanging or stopping a spear, but nothing else.

He spent an hour walking along the battlements adjoining the fort. The icy winds sweeping down the barren landscape from the north helped to clear his mind, and wipe away uncomfortable memories of the red-headed girl in his bed.

He leaned his elbows on the parapet, and thought of all the generations of Roman legionaries that had stood here, buffeted by winds and rain, watching nervously for any sign of the dreaded Picts, the Painted Ones, lurking among the heather.

They were drawn from all over the Empire, the soldiers who had guarded this Godforsaken spot, from the baking plains of North Africa to the frozen wastes of Scythia. For those raised in warmer climes, being sent to the Wall must have seemed a terrible punishment. To the Romans, this was the furthest frontier of the civilised world. Beyond lay nothing but rainy wilderness and scattered tribes of man-eating savages.

Ambrosius had been sent to ride into that wilderness. He peered into the misted landscape, obscured by drifting curtains of drizzle and fog, and wondered what awaited him.

In theory, the territory north of the Wall was guarded by certain local tribes, subjugated long ago by the Romans and paid to form an extra barrier against the Picts. Considering the number of times Pictish war-bands had swept down from their dark forested highlands and attacked the Wall, meeting with little resistance on the way, Ambrosius considered them a flimsy barrier at best.

The northern tribes were wild, every bit as wild as the painted savages they were hired to fight. Only a fool would trust them. Even so, Ambrosius was glad to leave Vercovicium and its sullen, uncooperative garrison, and venture into the unknown at the head of his men.

He expected the journey to be full of danger, but no hostile war-bands appeared on the horizon as they rode the forty miles to Curia. The stark beauty of the land was offset by rain, pelting down in sheets from grey skies shot through with ragged black clouds.

Ambrosius had grown used to being soaked while in the north country, but the rain here seemed to have a harder, more insidious quality. It seeped through his thick woollen cloak and the links of his mail and the folds of cloth and leather underneath. Standing still for any length of time presented a risk of drowning.

He wiped his streaming face and thought dreamily of blazing fires and hot food.

"On," he shouted, giving his reins a shake and urging his miserable, thoroughly wet horse on towards the mist-shrouded ridge of the fort.

The shadow of Curia loomed ominously above the horsemen as they neared the lower levels of its southern flank. About halfway up, Ambrosius could see a narrow path running around the hill, and above that a turf rampart faced with stone. He peered up at the summit, rising high, high above his head, and glimpsed thin trails of smoke rising from the settlement.

A few rooftops were visible, mere dots at this distance. He pictured the sentries on the wall, gazing down at the tiny figures of horsemen, far below, and debating whether or not to drop something on their heads.

Then his eye picked out a band of horsemen moving along the path at a canter. Twenty men, mounted on little hill-ponies, with a chief and a standard bearer at their head. The dusky evening light sparkled off the gold ornaments at the chief's head, wrists and throat, but the device on the standard was invisible, its cloth soaked through and drooping miserably in the wet.

Ambrosius gave the order to halt. The chief would be Cunedda, Lord of Curia and King of the Votadini, or one of his nobles. His small following suggested Cunedda meant to welcome Ambrosius, as did the lack of missiles raining down from above.

The horsemen swung off the path onto an even narrower trail, cut into the south side of the hill and leading straight down to its base. Their chief raised his spear in greeting as they rode within earshot.

"Lord Ambrosius," he cried, "at last you have come. My sentries thought your men were a pack of sheep, wandering aimlessly in the hills, but then they saw your banner. It is long since the dragon was seen in these parts. I am Cunedda."

Ambrosius greeted him politely in return, and suffered his hand to be crushed in the other man's bone-grinding grip.

He judged Cunedda to be about forty, a lean and wiry man with intelligent green eyes and bristling red hair. His greasy beard was knotted into a single plait flowing down to his waist, and his breath was foul. Ambrosius struggled not to gag as it rolled over him in hot, stinking gusts.

Twisting serpents of hammered gold shone at his wrists and throat, and a thin band of gold adorned his brow. Ambrosius was astonished to see him wearing an ancient sculpted Roman cuirasse over his mail, probably looted from the grave of a long-dead centurion.

Cuirasse and mail were painted gold, and patterns of blue swirling tattoos were visible under the torcs decorating his wrists and neck. Ambrosius suspected the man's body was covered in tattoos, reminding him disturbingly of the Pictish warriors he had seen at Deva.

Such was Cunedda, one of the most splendid barbarians Ambrosius had ever met, and certainly the most welcoming.

"We shall feast you until your guts are full to bursting," Cunedda declared, slapping his meaty hand on Ambrosius' back, "pour a sweet yellow flow of mead down your throat, and send you off to bed with a woman or two. Or three, or four, depending on your appetite, eh?"

Ambrosius muttered something about being a married man, but Cunedda didn't seem to hear him. He was a warlord to his roots, and not inclined to pay much attention to what others said.

The long line of horsemen made their way up the trail onto the path, which led west along the south face of the hill before curving around to meet a gatehouse on the south-west flank.

Night was advancing rapidly, as it always did in this part of the country, and the rain was coming down in almost solid waves. Ambrosius could barely see a hand's breath in front of him as the gates yawned open and he urged his dispirited mount into the darkness beyond.

He thought she had suffered quite enough, so climbed wetly off her back and led her through the gate on foot. He emerged to find a crowd of soaking barbarians waiting to greet him.

"My people," said Cunedda, "gathered here to do you honour. And, truth to tell, to gawp at you. We don't get many visitors, or encourage them."

The sea of bodies respectfully parted to let their master and his guests through. Ambrosius nodded and smiled politely at them, noting the fine dress of the warriors under their drenched cloaks, and the poor and ragged apparel of the common folk.

Harsh, craggy faces, seamed with dirt, stared back at him with eyes full of suspicion and ignorance. These were a hard people, taut for war, condemned to endure hard lives on the top of this desolate, wind-blown rock. The children far outnumbered the adults, a host of mucky, squealing brats, infesting the place like vermin.

The town on the summit was huge, even bigger than Ambrosius expected, and covered some thirty acres. He followed Cunedda up a rising stretch of ground, past untidy rows of thatched huts and roundhouses, onto a plateau. Here the largest dwellings stood in the teeth of the winds billowing in from the sea, a grey line just visible to the east.

Cunedda's mead-hall lay in the middle of the plateau, surrounded by a rough circle of smaller longhouses. The hall was built along the same lines as the one at Mons Ambrius, but much larger, and looked capable of housing at least two hundred warriors.

Ambrosius was grateful for the heat of the fire inside, burning merrily below an iron pot fixed to a chain suspended from the rafters. A couple of slaves tended the meat stew bubbling inside, while others heaped the food onto wooden platters and took them to the men seated at the mead-benches.

A great roar of welcome erupted from the throats of Cunedda's warriors, accompanied by the hammering of fists and knife-handles.

"Drink to the health of our guests!" roared Cunedda, snatching a horn full of bright yellow mead from a cringing slave, "drink to Ambrosius Aurelianus, son of the Consul, lord of Mons Ambrius, envoy from the court of the High King himself!"

He tossed down the mead, or most of it, in one swallow, while the rest slopped down his front. His warriors gleefully followed suit.

Ambrosius was offered a brimming horn by a tiny male slave, no more than five or six years old.

"Drink, lord," the boy piped when Ambrosius hesitated, "or else they will take it as an insult."

Ambrosius steeled himself and accepted the horn, noting absently that the boy was thin as a reed, and had a mop of dirty ash-blonde hair.

He managed to gulp half the mead, which was sickly sweet and thick as gravy. His performance was good enough for the

Votadini, who bellowed their approval, like a herd of excited oxen.

Head ringing, he allowed Cunedda to take him by the hand and lead him to his place beside the king's chair at high table.

More mead was served to him there, as well as a heaped platter of roast meat, slathered in glutinous brown sauce. Ambrosius' guts churned at the sight, but he was ever courteous, and sawed off a piece of the tough beef with his eating knife.

Meanwhile his men were given places at the lower tables, next to Cunedda's warriors, and the feast began in earnest. A harpist seated in a far corner started to pluck out a haunting melody, softening the babble of rough, drunken voices.

"My thanks for your hospitality, lord king," Ambrosius said after forcing down his bit of meat and gristle, "you know my mission."

Cunedda was already polishing off his third horn of ale. The things were impossible to set down, thanks to the curve of the horn, and had to be drained to avoid spillage. It was an easy way of getting very drunk very quickly.

"Of course," Cunedda replied after unleashing a loud belch, "messages have been going back and forth between here and Eburucum for the past few weeks. Coel Hen warned me of your coming."

Ambrosius chose his next words with care. "I am here," he said, "to help escort your people to their new home. Nothing more. Coel Hen assured me you were willing to comply with the Council's wishes."

He looked anxiously at Cunedda, trying to read his thoughts.

Cunedda grabbed a loaf of rye bread, twisted off a chunk, and chewed it for a while before replying. His eyes had taken on a distant look.

"My people have lived here for centuries," he said, "this was our home, long before the coming of Christ to these isles, or the first legions."

He glanced sidelong at Ambrosius, who knew better than to miss a cue.

"The council's offer stands," he replied, "in return for leaving your tribal lands and re-settling your people in Venedotia, you will be given all the lands in that region."

Cunedda raised a finger. "To rule as I see fit," he said firmly, "not as some damned praetor, or whatever dead Roman office the council might want to bind round my neck. Venedotia shall be my land, governed by all the laws and customs my people follow here."

"Agreed, lord king. Provided you keep your side of the bargain, and defend the coasts."

This was the meat of the mission Ambrosius had been despatched to fulfil. The number of Scotti raids on the western coast of Britannia were again on the rise. Desperate for warriors to defend the region, the Council of Britannia had thought of uprooting one of the tribes north of the Wall and moving them west.

Ambrosius' father first suggested the idea, and was instrumental in forcing Vortigern to agree to it. In the years since Guolpoh, Aurelius had turned peacemaker, and laboured to patch up a truce between his son and the High King. Having once

schemed to overthrow Vortigern and replace him as the supreme power in Britannia, he now thought only of a peaceful settlement.

Sending Ambrosius north in person was a way of easing the tension between the contending factions. Ambrosius appreciated this, but could not help feeling a twinge of resentment at being pushed aside. It smacked of demotion, as though Aurelius sought to steal back all the power and responsibility he had freely abdicated to his son prior to Guoloph.

Still, the policy of relocating the Votadini was a sensible one, and Ambrosius was glad to perform a useful service. He had left his wife and daughter at Mons Ambrius, where they were safe.

In his heart, he had to admit it was something of a relief to get away from his family. Morgana was now almost fifteen, and completely blind. The miraculous cure performed by Bishop Germanus had failed, as his wife said it would, and the poor girl destined for a convent.

Morgana's mere presence filled him with anger and shame: anger at the false promises of so-called holy men, and shame at himself, for fathering such a helpless creature. She would be his only child, since Helena was too old to risk bearing any more.

"The Votadini will fulfil their oath," said Cunedda, "we shall line the cliffs with the heads of Scotti pirates. In time, Venedotia shall become the most peaceful and prosperous kingdom in the isles, and I shall die as a man should."

"On the battlefield?" asked Ambrosius, who knew these barbarians set great store on meeting violent ends.

Cunedda was different. "God and the Saints preserve us, no," he replied, making the sign of the cross, "I mean to die rich, fat, and happy, surrounded by grieving women and a healthy litter of sons. I am unlikely to do so here. My enemies gather, Ambrosius, like carrion-birds round a dying calf. Curia is too strong for them to try and take by storm, but one day…"

His voice trailed off. Ambrosius knew of what he spoke. The Votadini were just one of the tribes scuffling for territory north of the Wall. They included the Selgovae and the Damnonii, as well as others he had forgotten the names of. Rome might have intended them to guard her northernmost frontier, but in recent years they had turned to fighting each other as well as the Picts.

"Move west, lord king," said Ambrosius, leaning in close to Cunedda, "the land is good there, and you can rule unchallenged."

Cunedda stared into the middle distance for a while longer, and then slapped his hand down on the table, making the bowls jump.

"I shall!" he cried, "to hell with this benighted lump of rock. Let my enemies have the place, and see how they like it. May God send them colds and fevers, and enough rain to drown them like the rats they are."

Ambrosius thought Cunedda would have to discuss the matter with his elders and nobles, but the tribe made ready for departure the very next morning. The word of their king was law, and the Votadini lived and died according to his wishes.

Excess of mead – it had proved impossible to avoid, as the feast wore on – had left Ambrosius with the inevitable skull-cracking headache, and he could do little save watch as the tribe packed up their belongings. His bowels were loose, and he was frequently obliged to rush to the row of latrine-pits behind the hall.

It was still raining, light showers dropping from a dull, overcast sky, but he found the wind and the rain helped him to recuperate. The air on the lofty summit of Curia was fresh, the purest he had ever tasted, and by noon he felt almost human again.

The Votadini worked fast, especially with Cunedda chivvying them like a furious shepherd, riding about on his grey pony and barking orders. His warriors removed their families and horses, followed by slaves driving wagons loaded with war-gear and other possessions. The common folk had little to carry, but were tasked with moving the tribe's herds of rather stringy cattle, sheep and goats, as well as the poultry.

Ambrosius stood leaning miserably against the doorway to the hall, wishing the pain in his head would dissolve. He had sent his men, most of them also nursing hangovers, to the plain below the fort, where they could recover in peace.

He watched the Votadini shuffle past. Young men herding their families before them, old men and women limping on sticks, women clutching babies, children carrying ducks and hens. There were dogs everywhere, hairy mongrel shapes, barking in excited confusion as they loped along the edges of the ragged procession.

Squabbles frequently broke out among the hot-blooded northerners, and sometimes came to blows. A couple of young girls started quarrelling over a baby not three feet in front of Ambrosius, screaming in each other's faces while the infant bawled at the top of its lungs.

Ambrosius couldn't stand it. He moved away, clutching his head with both hands, to look for a quiet spot round the corner of the hall, out of the wind.

Even here, there was no respite. He almost stumbled over three boys fighting on the ground behind the western wall. It was an unequal contest. The two bigger youths were holding down the smallest and frenziedly beating him to a pulp.

"What's this?" said Ambrosius, seizing the youths by their earlobes and dragging them off their victim, "two against one? For shame. What are your names, my heroes?"

The youths squealed and squirmed in his grip like frightened rabbits. He twisted harder when they failed to answer his question, and lifted them onto their toes.

"Bedwyr!" the black-haired one yelled, though his companion, a stocky redhead, remained obdurate.

Ambrosius released the redhead and cuffed him. "Your name," he growled, "or I'll hit you again."

The boy was knocked to the ground. "Cei," he replied sullenly, spitting out dirt and staring up at Ambrosius with murder in his eyes.

"Bedwyr and Cei," Ambrosius said severely, in his best drill-ground manner, "listen to me, and remember. Standard army punishment for assaulting a comrade is twenty lashes with a vine rod. Would you like bloody backs, lads? I have seen grown men scream for mercy under the rod."

The youths said nothing, though Bedwyr yelled again when Ambrosius gave his ear a final twist before letting him go.

He suddenly tired of playing the disciplinarian. What in God's name was he doing here, on the edge of the civilised world, trying to teach manners to wolf-cubs?

"Get out of my sight," he said, "and don't let me see you again. Cravens. You're not worth the effort of thrashing."

Cei's face flooded with angry blood, but Bedwyr grabbed his arm before he could do or say anything foolish. The pair loped off, casting puzzled and resentful glances over their shoulders at Ambrosius, before vanishing round the corner.

Their victim had already picked himself up, and was trying to wipe the mud from his already filthy tunic. His mop of ash-blonde hair was familiar.

"You're the slave who served me that disgusting mead last night," said Ambrosius, placing his index finger under the boy's chin and tilting it up to the light, "your friends gave you quite a beating."

This was an understatement, The boy's right eye was swelling up beautifully, as was his lower lip. Blood leaked from his nose, and lesser bruises marked his neck and the left side of his forehead. Judging by the marks on his throat, Cei and Bedwyr had made a spirited attempt to throttle him.

"What did you say to make them so angry?" asked Ambrosius, a sliver of pity cutting through his indifference. To be a slave, and a child-slave at that, in a pigsty like Curia, was one of the worst fates he could imagine.

The boy's clear blue eyes were dry, and he grinned, exposing bloodied teeth. "It was my fault," he said happily, "I said neither of them could beat me in a fight, even if they attacked me at the same time. That made them cross, especially Cei. He has a bad temper."

"Evidently," said Ambrosius, wincing as he gently probed the bruise on the boy's head. It would swell up into an unsightly lump, and make him look quite disfigured for days.

"You were extremely unwise," he added, "never take on overwhelming odds, lad, unless absolutely necessary. One of the first rules of war."

The boy shrugged. "Fighting is important. It makes me strong. My father was a warrior. He bade me fight."

"And who is your father? I should like to speak with him."

"He is nobody. Not anymore. When he was alive, his name was Uthyr, but now he is dead."

The boy spoke of his father's death quite carelessly, as though it didn't matter to him. Ambrosius was intrigued.

"How did he die?"

"In battle. He was a warrior of the Selgovae, but one day the Votadini came and burned our village. They slew all the men, and took the women and children as slaves."

"Including your mother?" Ambrosius asked gently.

The boy wiped his bleeding nose, and nodded.

"Yes. She died too, not long after. I don't remember her very well. I was very young. Most of the slaves died. The Votadini are not kind. But I am still alive."

AMBROSIUS

He puffed out his shallow chest, like a tiny bird of prey, and looked absurdly pleased with himself. For the first time since he ventured north of the Wall, Ambrosius laughed.

Oh, for a son like this, he thought, and instantly regretted doing so. In an obscure sort of way, it felt like a betrayal of Helena.

"What is your name, last champion of the Selgovae?" he asked, trying and failing to sound stern.

The boy gazed up at him fearlessly.

"Artúir," came the reply.

15.

Hengist stood in the centre of a ring of torches, under the mighty, eons-old silhouette of the stones, and seized Vortigern's wrist.

The High King offered no resistance as the Saxon swept his hand up into the air.

"All hail Vortigern," Hengist cried, "all hail the High King of the Britons."

His cry was echoed by the tightly-packed ring of men standing around him. Fifty, in all, the twenty-four members of the Council of Britannia, and a roughly equal number of Saxon chiefs.

Every man in the ring held aloft a torch, but carried no weapons. They had all come to this assembly, held inside the ancient henge near Mons Ambrius, unarmed and accompanied by just one servant each. Only the nobles were allowed in the central cluster of stones, and so left their servants and horses outside.

The assembly was Hengist's idea, one he had put to Vortigern months previously.

"We must have peace in the land, lord king," he said, "there is no need for this animosity between your people and mine."

"There can be no peace," Vortigern replied gloomily, "until I am dead, or Aurelius and his allies are dead. The hatred between our factions has gone too deep. Such roots cannot ever be torn out."

Hengist brushed aside the High King's pessimism. He was Vortigern's chief policy-maker now, as well as Magister Militum of his army of Saxon mercenaries. Though he continued to show his royal brother-in-law respect in public, and address him as lord, there was no doubt which of them held the reins of power.

"I propose a truce," he said, meaning he ordered one, "since the councillors are too afraid of my people to come to Londinium, let us meet somewhere more acceptable to them."

"Somewhere sacred, perhaps," he added, warming to his theme, "where their ancestors worshipped."

In the end they had decided on the henge, right in the heart of Britannia, near the headquarters of Ambrosius and the site of the slaughter of Guoloph.

"Perfect," said Hengist, rubbing his hands, "what better place to sign a treaty of eternal peace and friendship between Saxon and Briton?"

For once he took Vortigern into his confidence, hiding nothing from the ageing High King, and soon afterwards riders were sent out from Londinium, to summon the absent councillors to the assembly.

Hengist was delighted by the response. Every single member of the council was present, even old Aurelius, who had spent much of his life in bitter opposition to Vortigern.

Disappointingly, Ambrosius did not attend. "My son is far to the north, lord king," Aurelius had informed Vortigern after the most perfunctory of bows, "in Venedotia, inspecting the coastal defences."

Hengist spoke before the High King could reply. "Your son appears to have made quite a friend in Cunedda," he said, "Ambrosius has always been shrewd in his choice of friends."

Something of Aurelius' old fire sparked in his eyes as he glared at Hengist.

"I wish I could say the same for Vortigern," he answered curtly, and showed the Saxon his back.

Hengist smiled faintly as he watched the Consul stump away. His brother Horsa, standing immediately to his right, made a growling noise in the back of his throat.

"Peace, brother," he said quietly, "let him be. This is a peace conference, remember?"

Horsa slowly subsided. The giant Saxon chief was still a formidable prospect, though the years, and the appalling wounds he suffered at Guoloph, had sapped some of his brute strength and energy. His hair was prematurely white, and the spear-wound to his stomach rendered him incapable of digesting solid food. He was forced to live on soup and a sort of paste, made from meat and vegetables ground up together.

If Horsa was diminished, Hengist had only grown in confidence and authority. He looked to his left, beyond the stooped, greying figure of Vortigern to Pascent, the only one of the king's sons to attend. The others still resided on their mother's estates.

Hiding behind her skirts, he thought scornfully.

Pascent stared straight ahead, deliberately ignoring Hengist's gaze. He was a dutiful young man, if not overly bright. Hengist had insisted on his presence at the assembly. The more royal blood, the better.

It was a warm spring night, and Hengist savoured the taut atmosphere inside the stones, the almost tangible sense of fear and distrust, before speaking again.

"We have summoned you all here," he said, raising his voice, "to talk of peace. My friends, Britannia is threatened by enemies on all sides. Now we hear of stirrings in Gaul, of the revival of Roman power under a general named Flavius Aetius. He has already inflicted great slaughter on the Visigoths and reclaimed large portions of Roman territory. How long before he turns his eyes west? How long before he thinks of leading his victorious armies over the sea, to reclaim Britannia for the Western Empire?"

He paused for breath. Silence reigned inside the circle, broken only by the gentle flapping of Vortigern's eagle banner. A light breeze drifted through, causing the flames of the torches to flicker and cast grotesque shadows against the stones.

"With all this in mind," he continued, "there can be no question of the necessity of peace. Only together, united against all these threats, can we hope to survive and prosper."

He looked straight at Aurelius, whose craggy face was creased with suspicion.

"Has our ruler lost his tongue?" barked the Consul, "let him speak for himself."

Vortigern didn't seem to hear his old rival, but stared listlessly at the ground, lost in thought. He made for a wizened, uninspiring figure, bent under the weight of years.

"As for the High King," Hengist said smoothly, "I speak for him. He only desires a peaceful land, and to see our peoples united against their common foes."

"My common foe stands before me," snarled Aurelius, "and I tire of his yelping. Let the High King speak, or I shall quit this assembly."

His chief allies, Lucius Septimius and Flavius Sanctus, grunted in agreement. They were old men now, and Lucius was obliged to walk with a stick, but remained constant in their opposition to Vortigern.

The lights of Mons Ambrius glinted to the west. If Aurelius chose to leave, he only had to make a two-mile journey to the safety of his son's headquarters.

Hengist had no intention of allowing him to depart. "Enough of this petty bickering," he shouted, raising Vortigern's hand again, "my friends, I ask you once more to hail the High King. Honour him!"

These last words were a pre-arranged signal. As soon as they fell from his lips, the Saxons inside the circle drew their saexes, hidden under their tunics or in the soles of their shoes, and went to work.

The Britons had come in good faith, and were taken completely unawares. Screams and oaths erupted inside the ancient circle as the Saxons revealed their treachery. The ground, once liberally wetted with the blood of pagan sacrifices, was now soaked again in gore as the long-bladed saexes stabbed and thrust into unprotected bodies.

Hengist watched in silent glee as the councillors were pitilessly murdered before his eyes. None carried weapons, and could only defend themselves with bare hands against the terrible knives.

Vortigern did not move or speak as the massacre was carried out. He knew all about it. Only by removing the councillors, Hengist had persuaded him, could he hope to recover his authority and rule as a High King should.

His son Pascent, being far too honourable and stupid to be trusted, knew nothing of the plan. He cried out in horror as the blades flashed into life, but was seized by Horsa and wrapped up in the giant's powerful arms.

"Be calm, my prince," said Hengist as the young man kicked and struggled uselessly against Horsa's iron grip, "you and your father will come to no harm."

The killing was a messy business, and went on for some time. Cadeyrn, the hugely fat and virtually crippled King of the Durotriges, was tipped out of his chair and squealed like a frightened child as tried to crawl to safety. Two of Hengist's men dragged him over to one of the gigantic bluestone monoliths and dashed his brains out against its lichen-covered base.

Vortigern had suggested Cadeyrn and one or two of the other loyal councillors might be spared, but Hengist was adamant. It had to be a thorough job. The survivors would only cause trouble.

Many of the Britons made shameful ends, begging and whining for mercy even as the saexes bit into their flesh, but a few made a fight of it.

Aurelius was one. He caught the wrist of the Saxon who stabbed at him, and tried to twist the saex out of his attacker's grasp. Another Saxon leaped in from behind and buried his blade up to the hilt in his kidneys. He gasped and threw back his head, mouth gaping in noiseless agony.

His first assailant's saex slashed across his throat. Eyes wide, blood spurting from the fatal wound, Aurelius crumpled to the ground.

"Long overdue," remarked Hengist as he watched the Consul jerk in his death-throes. The old men, Lucius and Flavius were next to die, held down and stabbed repeatedly.

Hengist glanced sidelong at Vortigern, expecting some reaction, but the High King's eyes were shut.

He grinned. Vortigern could feign being deaf and dumb to this night's work, if he liked, but would never escape the consequences.

When all was done, and the last dying scream had faded away, Hengist wandered among the slain, occasionally stooping to turn a body over and study its face.

"Twenty-three," he said at last, straightening and wiping his bloody hands on his cloak, "one is missing."

"Eidol Cadarn, lord," replied Guechta, whose burly frame was smeared from head to toe in blood, "the magistrate of Glevum. He and his servant escaped."

Hengist was displeased. Eidol Cadarn was an important British noble, and ruled one of the few remaining occupied Roman towns in the west. As such he was well-placed to join forces with Ambrosius, should the latter seek him for an ally.

Otherwise, the results of Hengist's treachery were most satisfactory. In a few short minutes, the Council of Britannia had been annihilated, leaving the way clear for the next stage of his grand scheme.

He returned to Vortigern and Pascent, carefully stepping over the sprawled body of Aurelius on the way.

Pascent's face was a tear-streaked mask of horror. "You animal," he whispered, hanging limply in Horsa's grip, "you filthy, murdering pagan animal. You will burn in Hell for all eternity."

"Perhaps," Hengist said indifferently, "but first I shall rule on earth. Stop blubbering, you little fool. What manner of prince are you? Your weakness makes me sick."

He turned to Vortigern, who was now leaning against the altar-stone, staring dumbly at the blood-flecked grass.

Has he lost his reason? thought Hengist, frowning. All false deference forgotten, he reached out and jerked the High King's head up.

A pair of terrified eyes stared back at him. Vortigern's lips worked, and he mumbled something inaudible.

Hengist spread his arm to indicate the slaughtered councillors.

"See, lord king?" he said, gently patting Vortigern's cheek, "your enemies are no more."

The other man's face turned a ghastly shade of grey, and his teeth audibly chattered as he gazed at the dead.

"My…my enemies," he stammered, "my…my…my…"

Hengist grasped his hand again and held it high. "All hail our tame High King!" he laughed, turning to face his blood-soaked followers, "all hail Vortigern, our slave-king!"

The Saxons laughed with him, and raised their dripping saexes in mock salute.

"All hail the slave-king!" they shouted, *"the slave-king!"*

16.

Artúir grew up quickly. In later years, whenever he had the leisure to reflect on his childhood, it seemed an endless series of sudden terrors and alarms.

Not that he regretted a moment of it. The blood of generations of northern warriors ran in his veins, and from an early age he strove to live up to his ancestry.

Artúir's memories of his parents were vague and confused, and caused him little joy. His father, Uthyr, he remembered as a towering black-bearded monster, his hard body covered in scars.

"You must fight as often as possible, my son," Uthyr had told him, "men should fight. A man who won't fight is worth nothing. When you grow up, you will be a warrior like me, perhaps even lead your own war-band one day. You will grow strong, and other men will be afraid of you."

These were Uthyr's last words to him, before the Votadini came and smashed Artúir's world to pieces. He remembered flames, people screaming as they died, and blades flashing in the darkness.

He could also remember the bite of the leather thongs on his wrists, when the Votadini took him and his mother away as slaves.

His mother, Ygraine, was an enduring puzzle. She had loved Uthyr with a passion bordering on madness, but didn't seem to love their only child at all. Other men had tender memories of their mothers, but all he could remember of Ygraine was a thin-faced woman with long auburn hair, who looked at Artúir with resentment and gave him naught but hard blows and cold words.

"God took my beloved," she would say, "and left you. Why? Why didn't he take you instead? I could have borne Uthyr more sons, but I will never find another man like him."

She had little use for life without Uthyr, and soon ended it. Shortly after they and the rest of the slaves from the raid were brought to Curia, she was found hanging from the rafters of one of the cattle-byres.

"Cut that thing down," ordered Cunedda, the lord of Curia, "and take it into the forest, far from here. I'll not have the body of a suicide on my land."

Artúir was left alone. Somehow he survived the following winter, clinging to life with grim determination, while his fellow slaves died like flies. They were treated like animals, given the worst food to eat and made to sleep in the outhouses with the livestock. Beatings were common, especially when Cunedda and his warriors were in their cups, and more than one slave died under the whip.

"A man who won't fight is worth nothing," Uthyr had said, and his son took him at his word. Artúir intended to fight, not just on the battlefield, but for everything: the right to live, to escape the shame of slavery, to win the respect of others.

Everything changed when the Roman came to Curia. Ambrosius, they called him, a tall man with severely cropped black hair, a lean face and sad eyes.

From the moment Ambrosius stepped into Cunedda's hall, Artúir found him fascinating. He was clean-shaven, which was unusual for a man, and carried himself with a quiet, unassuming dignity.

He accepted the drinking horn full of mead Artúir offered him with grave courtesy, and stepped around the boy instead of simply walking through him, as Artúir was used to and expected.

For the rest of the evening, Artúir kept to the shadows of Cunedda's hall and watched Ambrosius. The Roman picked at his meat, and tried to drink sparingly, though Cunedda insisted on pressing a constant supply of mead and ale on him. His manner was reserved, and he spoke low in Cunedda's ear, with none of the drunken boisterousness and flamboyant gestures of the northern warriors seated around him.

His men were almost as reticent as their chief, though a few relaxed as the evening wore on, and joined in with the singing and drinking games. Artúir noticed their sober, almost drab appearance, lacking the tattoos, piercings and ornaments the Votadini loved to adorn themselves with, and the superior quality of their armour and weapons. Every one of Ambrosius' men wore a mail shirt, well-oiled and polished and gleaming in the light from the fire, and carried a long sword.

Among the Votadini, only Cunedda and the chief warriors of his *teulu* wore mail. Artúir's father had gone to war protected by nothing more than a small round shield and a leather shirt with a few pieces of bone sewn onto it by Ygraine.

When the feast was coming to an end, Artúir crept out of the hall and made his way to the nearest byre, where he lay among the soft, dry hay and thought of Ambrosius. One of his favourite dogs, a lean black and white mongrel bitch he had named Gyflym after her great speed, lay beside him.

The Roman, he decided, would rescue him from slavery. That was the reason God had brought him to Curia.

Once Artúir's mind was settled on an idea, he rarely experienced doubts or second thoughts. Satisfied, he wrapped his arms around Gyflym's warm body, burrowed down into the hay and fell asleep.

He was woken by the damp muzzle of a cow, snuffling in his hair, and her rough tongue licking his face. Artúir pushed her away, yawned, stretched until the bones clicked, and made his way outside into the bright new morning. Gyflym trotted at his heels.

Few minded what he did or where he went, so long as he was on hand in the evenings to serve meat and drink. A slave of Artúir's tender years wasn't good for much else.

His belly rumbled. As usual, he was hungry, and so returned to the hall, knowing there would be plenty of scraps and leftovers from the feast.

He peered carefully through the door. The hall was full of sleeping warriors, some of them passed out at the tables, others wrapped up on the floor in their cloaks. A familiar stench of stale ale, unwashed bodies and flatulence filled Artúir's nostrils.

"Stay here," he said softly, placing his hand on Gyflym's muzzle, "and be quiet. I'll find a nice bone for you."

The dog whined, but sat obediently while Artúir soft-footed into the hall, carefully picking his way through the snoring bodies.

None of them woke as his tiny shape flitted through the musty semi-darkness. The best way for a slave to survive was to avoid being noticed, and Artúir had made himself an expert at moving swiftly and silently.

He snatched some half-chewed meat bones from one of the tables, a jug of mead and a few bits of bread, and followed his steps back to the doorway, his arms laden with plunder.

"Here," he said, tossing Gyflym one of the bones. She followed him around the side of the hall, to a quiet spot out of the wind, where he could eat his stolen breakfast in peace.

He loved to sit here and gaze at the sea, some five miles to the east. To Artúir, the sea was freedom. He often liked to picture himself as one of the sea-rovers whose boats were occasionally glimpsed off the coasts. They were like wild geese, driven by the wind, free to come and go as they pleased.

Gyflym laid her head on Artúir's lap, her gold-flecked eyes staring up at him.

"If the Roman does not free me," he said, stroking her sleek head, "I will run away to sea. You can come too. We shall find a boat and beg the sea-wolves to take us with them."

He stayed here for over an hour, his eyes fixed on the sea, mulling over glorious futures in his head while the town woke up around him.

There was more noise than usual. Men shouting, children crying, women complaining. Cunedda's harsh voice rose above it all, barking orders. Artúir paid little heed to the din. The Votadini were not his people, and their doings were of no concern to him. One day soon, he would be free of them, and this hilltop prison.

"Here he is," said a familiar, hateful voice, breaking in on his thoughts, "the little slave and his lover. Is it true what they say, Artúir? Do the Selgovae lie with animals? Was your father a dog?"

Cei's voice. Fear pumped through Artúir's chest as he glanced to his left and saw the tall, rangy, red-headed youth, and his friend Bedwyr, sauntering towards him.

They were both a few years his senior, the sons of Votadini warriors. Ever since Artúir was brought to Curia they had picked him out for special treatment.

Of the two, Cei was the worst, and delighted in inflicting pain. Artúir had lost count of the number of times the bigger boy had made him eat dirt, pinning him face-down to the ground and twisting his arms behind his back. Artúir always did his best not to cry out – that only made Cei hurt him more – but could only endure the pain so long.

Gyflym knew them of old, and had often been on the receiving end of Cei's foot. She whimpered at the sight of him and galloped away, leaving Artúir to his fate.

"Sensible beast," Cei laughed, "you should run as well. Go on, run!"

Artúir stood up and pressed his short back against the wall. They were both looming over him now, almost twice his size, eyes glittering with malice. He knew what was coming, and braced himself.

"Won't run," he muttered stubbornly. He was mortally afraid, but would rather die than show it.

"What's that?" said Bedwyr, whose darkly handsome face formed a vivid contrast to his freckled, snub-nosed companion, "you won't run? Just as well. You wouldn't get very far on those short little legs."

Bedwyr's hands shot out and gripped Artúir's throat, lifting him up off the ground. Artúir gasped for breath, kicking and struggling, purple spots flashing before his eyes. He thought he was going to die.

"Put him on the grass," said Cei, rolling up the sleeves of his tunic. Sniggering, Bedwyr threw Artúir onto his back and kicked him in the stomach.

Artúir had suffered these beatings before, and learned to roll with the blows. He tried to curl up into a ball, protecting his head with his hands, but Cei pinned his arms flat while Bedwyr sat astride his chest and rained punches down on his face.

"Dirty slave whelp," sneered Cei, "why don't you call for aid? Go on, try it. See who comes to save you."

Artúir refused to say anything, so Cei hit him in the mouth. The sight of blood welling over Artúir's lip seemed to excite him. He went to work in earnest, driving his fist down again and again, until his victim's face was a bleeding mask of pain.

Then the beating stopped. The eyes of his tormentors filled with astonishment as someone lifted them off their prey, and Artúir found himself looking up at the Roman.

It was glorious, the first victory of Artúir's life, to watch Cei and Bedwyr squirm in Ambrosius' grip. Now it was their turn to writhe helplessly against one who was stronger than they, and cower at his threats.

"Standard army punishment", said Ambrosius in the voice of a soldier, hard and pitiless, "for assaulting a comrade is twenty lashes with a vine rod. Would you like bloody backs, lads? I have seen grown men scream for mercy under the rod."

When they had gone, fleeing like a couple of whipped hounds, Ambrosius spoke to him gently, and asked him questions. Wanting to impress his saviour, Artúir lied that he had challenged Cei and Bedwyr to a fight, and was gratified when Ambrosius appeared to believe it.

He treasured that memory, and his memories of the following weeks. Often, during the long journey to Venedotia, Ambrosius called Artúir to his side and spoke with him in a serious sort of way, with none of the wanton cruelty and disdain the boy had come to expect from adults.

Ambrosius spoke of many things, most of them a complete mystery to Artúir: the history of the Romans in Britannia and the splendid things they had created, the evil of the High King, Vortigern, and his Saxon mercenaries.

Artúir was far more interested in his knowledge of military matters, and asked him endless questions about armour, weapons and horses, and how they waged war in the south. The Roman humoured his interest and gave him detailed answers, firing Artúir's imagination with images of mounted warriors in shining mail, riding to battle under a dragon banner.

Cunedda was clearly baffled by Ambrosius' behaviour. "Why do you bother with that slave brat?" Artúir overheard him saying one evening while he served them mead around the campfire, "if you're so fond of little boys, I can soon find you one with more meat on him."

Ambrosius ignored the coarse jest, and the laughter of Cunedda's warriors.

"I have no son," he replied, sitting cross-legged and gazing into his cup, "and the boy is without a father. We are equally bereft."

"Then take him," said Cunedda with a shrug, "my people do not lack for slaves, and can stand the loss of one stripling. Let him be my gift to you."

Artúir revolted at the notion of being passed about, like an animal or a piece of baggage, but he was glad to escape the Votadini.

Ambrosius proved a much gentler master. When he left Venedotia, he took Artúir with him, to the green and gentle southlands.

Mons Ambrius became Artúir's new home. First and foremost a military camp, Artúir spent his days in the company of soldiers. His eyes missed nothing, every detail of their trade, and he strived to make himself useful: cheerfully spending long hours cleaning rusted mail in hot water and vinegar, polishing swords and spear-heads, fletching arrows, performing any menial task that needed doing.

He loved horses. Ambrosius had created a paddock outside the fort, a flattish plain roughly half a mile square, enclosed by a timber fence. Here his growing stock of young foals were broken in and trained to serve as cavalry mounts. Whenever he could, Artúir perched on the fence and watched the animals being put through their paces.

His soul kindled at the sight of the cavalry at their drill, exercising with javelin and spatha, wheeling and manoeuvring to the sound of the bugle and the shouts of their officers.

Sometimes Ambrosius came and watched with him. "You want to be a horse-soldier," he said on one occasion, smiling down at the boy.

"More than anything," Artúir replied eagerly, "when I am big enough, I shall ride and fight as one of your buccelari."

"Careful. Unless I can find more men, and quickly, I may hold you to that promise sooner than you think."

Ambrosius spoke lightly, but there was a hollow note to his voice. His men were few, and Artúir sometimes heard them speak in low voices of a terrible battle, years before, where many of their comrades had died.

He saw little of Helena, Ambrosius' wife, one of the few women living at the fort. She spent much of her time inside the hall, a smaller version of Cunedda's mead-hall at Curia, or at prayer inside the wooden chapel Ambrosius had built nearby.

"She prays for her daughter," one of the soldiers Artúir had befriended told him, "the girl is blind, poor lass, and her parents had to put her away."

"Put her away?" said Artúir, his vivid imagination conjuring up an image of Ambrosius and Helena weeping as they buried their daughter alive.

"Yes, in a cloister. They couldn't find any man willing to marry a cripple, and so gave her to the church. Morgana, her name is. Lady Helena sometimes goes to visit her."

The soldier gave a sad little shake of his head. "Not her husband, though. Lord Ambrosius prefers to forget he has a daughter. Damned if I could treat any child of mine like that, but there it is. The world is cruel."

Artúir needed no lessons in cruelty. He had known nothing else until Ambrosius came to Curia and showed him a little kindness. It seemed strange to him, almost impossible, that the same man should not be kind to his own child.

There was something mysterious and unknowable about Ambrosius. The deep reserve Artúir had first noticed in him grew deeper over the following years. He was a sombre, distant figure, respected but not loved by his soldiers, and the weight of time and duty hung heavy on his narrow shoulders.

Ambrosius was often away from his headquarters, often for weeks at a time, supervising the building of the massive set of defensive fortifications north of Mons Ambrius, or visiting his allies. Cunedda was one of the latter. The two men, who could not be more different, had nevertheless become fast friends during the journey to Venedotia.

He was absent in the north when Vortigern held his great parley inside the stone circle, not two miles from Mons Ambrius. Artúir stood on the rampart and stared at the distant torch-light, flickering inside the mighty shadow of the monoliths, and wondered at what was being said.

"I want to see the High King," he complained, "and these Saxons everyone speaks of. I have never seen a Saxon. Not up close."

"You will see enough of them," growled the soldier standing to his left, "when you serve in the buccelari. Vicious hairy barbarians, and pagans to a man. Fit for nothing but a spear in the guts and a shallow grave."

"Why does Vortigern value them so highly, then?"

"Because he's a fool," the soldier replied shortly, "and a traitor to boot."

He seemed nervous and disinclined to talk, so Artúir said nothing more. Ambrosius had left the fort well-manned, and the upper rampart was lined with spearmen and archers, anxiously awaiting the outcome of the assembly.

It was difficult to tell from such a distance, but after a time the lights inside the stones appeared to flicker and merge. Artúir sensed the sudden tension in the man to his left, and thought he overheard faint screams, carried on the gentle night breeze.

"Did you hear it?" he asked. The soldier, his face ashen, gave a curt nod.

"Treachery," he whispered.

The captain of the garrison was a cautious man. His orders were to remain inside the fort, and he stuck to them.

He should muster the garrison and ride to the stones, thought Artúir, exasperated by the man's timidity, *and I with them.*

A wild impulse seized him. One of Ambrosius' horse-trainers had been teaching him to ride, slowly at first, leading a pony in a circle round the paddock while Artúir perched on the animal's back.

Artúir's people, the Selgovae, were skilled horsemen, and he came from a long line of horse-soldiers. Blood told, and he soon progressed to riding alone, without leading reins, though Ambrosius refused to let him tackle the big cavalry horses just yet.

He left the walkway and ran down the timber steps to the inner ward. There were plenty of horses stabled beside the hall. Artúir would take one and ride out to the stones by himself. If there was treachery, he would put a stop to it.

The thought briefly flitted across his mind that he was still a child, and carried no weapons save an eating knife. Artúir dismissed it. If he was marked to die, then at least he would make a good end, and be greeted warmly by his father's shade in Heaven.

He was halfway to the stables when a horn sounded on the rampart over the northern gate.

"Two riders!" he heard the sentry shout, "heading this way. They call for aid."

The looming shapes of men and horses burst out of the darkness. Artúir was almost ridden down as they thundered past him.

They were led by Longinus, the captain of the garrison, at the head of ten buccelari. Artúir watched them gallop towards the northern gate, where they dismounted and ran up the steps to the rampart.

Intrigued, Artúir forgot about his one-man rescue mission and followed them. None of the soldiers clustered on the walls gave his short, sturdy figure a second glance. Their eyes were fixed on the pair of horsemen galloping furiously across the shadowy plains to the east.

"Fugitives," said Longinus, shading his eyes to peer through the dark, "riding for their lives, though I see no pursuit. Wait! I recognise the man in front. Eidol Cadarn, magistrate of Glevum."

He leaned over the timber battlements to shout at the guards on the gatehouse defending the lower rampart.

"Open the gates!"

Artúir possessed an excellent memory for names. Since arriving at Mons Ambrius he had made it his business to learn as much as possible of Britannia and her rulers, and never ceased asking questions and listening to the soldiers talk.

Eidol Cadarn, he recalled, was the British magistrate of Glevum, an important town to the north of Mons Ambrius. He had a seat on the Council of Britannia, and would have been invited to the assembly at the stones.

The man who was admitted to the lower gate, and then the inner ward, bore little resemblance to one of the most wealthy and powerful nobles in Britannia. His face was pallid, his eyes rolling with terror, and his white tunic and grey cloak liberally splashed in blood. He rode bent double over his horse's neck, whimpering like a frightened hound, his fingers white as they clenched the reins.

Longinus and two of his men helped the stricken man out of the saddle. Eidol's servant, a young boy not much older than Artúir, was also smeared in blood, but seemed much less effected than his master.

"Wine," snapped Longinus, "and plenty of it. Quickly!" One of his soldiers ran off to fetch wine from the hall. Meanwhile Longinus tried to extract some sense from Eidol, who sat on the ground with his back against the gatehouse wall, clutching his head in both hands.

"My lord," said Longinus, kneeling next to him, "what happened at the stones? Does the High King live?" Eidol's ashen lips trembled as he tried to form words. "Knives," he whispered, slowly rocking to and fro, "knives in the dark. All gone!"

"Gone?" Longinus looked baffled. "What do you mean?"

He recoiled when Eidol lifted his head. Even Artúir took a step back. The magistrate's face was bone-white and drained of blood, and his bulging eyes had the look of one who had stared into the pit of Hell.

"The Council of Britannia," he muttered, "all gone. Dead. Destroyed. The Saxons murdered us all. Honour him! That was their cry. And then the knives came out. I ran. Like a coward. I ran, and lived while others died."

"All?" said Longinus, "what of the Consul, Aurelius? What of Vortigern?"

"Aurelius…he is gone, like the others…gone into shadow…"

Eidol's head dropped again, and Longinus could get no more sense out of him until the soldier returned with a flask of wine.

He was accompanied by Helena. Artúir had not seen Ambrosius' wife at close quarters before. She was hard-faced and painfully thin, old before her time, her grey hair severely combed back and bound up into a bun.

"Why is this man languishing out here?" she demanded in her cold, shrewish voice, "bring him into the hall. He needs warmth and light, and hot water to wash his wounds." "Did you hear me?" she said, staring angrily at the soldiers when they hesitated to obey, "I am your commander's wife. Do as I say!"

She held no real authority at the fort, but Longinus wisely gave way, and ordered his men to carry Eidol inside.

Artúir was left alone with Eidol's servant. "He owes me his life," said the latter, "small thanks I get for it."

He sounded amused rather than aggrieved. Artúir turned to look at him. He was a big, heavy-featured youth, with curling russet hair, brawny arms and a deep chest.

"I am Gwalchmai," he said, sliding easily off his pony, "I killed my first Saxon tonight. He tried to stab my master, so I picked up a stick off the ground and hit him on the head."

He grinned, and tapped his brow. "Wore no helmet, see? His skull burst like an egg. Mother always said I was too strong for my own good. Who are you?"

Artúir looked him up and down before replying. "My name is Artúir," he said, wrinkling his nose, "you stink of blood."

"Do I?" Gwalchmai glanced down at the splashes of red on his tunic. "There was a lot of blood. British, most of it. The Saxons hid their long knives inside their clothing. Clever bastards."

Gwalchmai seemed entirely unruffled by the massacre he had witnessed. "I should stable my pony, and rub her down," he said, patting the shuddering beast's neck, "she had a bad fright. Then I must attend my master."

"Follow me," said Artúir, who had taken a liking to the other boy, and led him towards the stables.

Ambrosius returned from the north five days later. By then Longinus and his men had retrieved the corpses of the British dead from the henge, and buried most of them in specially dug graves beside the chapel.

All save one. The body of Aurelius was washed clean of blood and laid out on the long table in the hall, to await the arrival of his son.

"It's high summer," remarked Gwalchmei, "let us hope Ambrosius is not long in coming, or the stink in there will be unbearable."

Artúir thought he should show more respect, but said nothing. He had never made a friend before. Gwalchmei seemed an easy-going sort, and content to amble around the fort in Artúir's company, listening to the younger boy talk.

"Ah, you're a northerner," he said when Artúir had spoken of his origins, "from beyond the Wall. That's interesting. Father told me they are all savages up there. Man-eaters, too. Do your people really eat their dead?"

"That's the Picts," replied Artúir, "they are the true savages. They still worship the old gods. My folk are all Christians."

Gwalchmei looked unconvinced. "My father is Eidol's cousin," he explained, "he used to be a soldier, and was posted at the Wall for a time. He swears the northern tribes are just as bad as the Picts. Not to be trusted."

Artúir could scarcely argue with that. His own people, the Selgovae, were notorious robbers and cattle thieves, and much preferred fighting to farming. He had a dim suspicion that the Votadini had attacked his village in reprisal for earlier raids carried out by the Selgovae.

He and his new friend stood on the walkway of the gatehouse and watched Ambrosius approach from the north. His dragon banner was clearly visible, and he rode at a canter, followed by sixty of his buccelari.

"So that's Ambrosius," said Gwalchmei, "I have heard much about him. Perhaps he already knows of the massacre. The whole of Britannia will know of it soon."

Helena and Longinus were waiting below, surrounded by a gathering of soldiers and priests, to receive their lord and give him the terrible news. Eidol also stood among them. He was somewhat recovered, thanks to Helena's nursing, though his eyes still had a hunted look.

The tall, spare figure of Ambrosius rode up the path to the gatehouse. Artúir studied him closely and thought Gwalchmei was right. He did look ill, and tired. His lean face had acquired a greyish pallor, and he rode stiffly, braced upright against nausea or exhaustion. Maybe both.

Helena held the reins of her husband's horse as he stiffly dismounted, and embraced him. He clung to her for a long moment.

"Come," Artúir overheard her say. She took his hand, and the ranks of the crowd parted to let the couple through. Helena led her husband as though he was a child, and he followed her with weary, plodding steps to the hall.

That evening Artúir received an unexpected summons. "Ambrosius wants to see you," said Longinus, who found the boys in the stables, rubbing down Gwalchmei's pony with wisps of straw, "don't ask me why, because he didn't tell me. Go!"

Artúir hurried to the hall, which he found empty save for the corpse laid out on the table. He held his nose. The heat was starting to have a bad effect on the earthly remains of Aurelius, as Gwalchmei said it would.

He paused for a moment to look at the body. Aurelius' eyes were closed, his fleshy features composed, almost serene in death. He was wrapped up in a fur-trimmed cloak, and a scarf covered his throat, discreetly hiding the wound that killed him.

"Artúir," said Ambrosius, "come here."

The heavy purple curtain at the eastern end of the hall was drawn back. Ambrosius' private chamber lay beyond.

He sat on a couch, Helena standing by his side, her hand resting on his shoulder. Artúir obediently walked over to them, noting Ambrosius' sickly pallor and the dark smudges under his eyes.

Ambrosius made no effort to hide or wipe away the tears coursing down his sallow cheeks.

"You and I share a common trait, Artúir," he said huskily, "we have both lost our fathers."

"See that," he added, lifting his right arm and pointing at Aurelius, "and remember the treachery of the Saxons. Never forget."

"I won't," said Artúir. Unable to think of anything more to say, he shifted awkwardly and studied the soft, richly decorated carpet under his feet. Helena had insisted on some civilised refinements, and covered the rough earthen floor of the chamber with costly rugs and carpets, taken from her old home in Londinium.

"The Saxons took my father," said Ambrosius, "while God saw fit to deny me a son. I will not abide by God's judgment. He has abandoned me, and my country, and thrown my people to the sea-wolves. Therefore we must shift for ourselves."

"Only if you are certain, my love," said Helena. Ambrosius laid his hand over hers.

"You are the son I should have fathered," he said, his pain-filled eyes fixed on Artúir, "and I intend to make you my son. I will raise you as my own and train you in the arts of war. You shall be Britannia's spear and shield, and keep her safe when I am gone. Forget your past, and your old name. You shall have a good Roman name instead."

He reached out and took Artúir's hand. "My adopted son. Artorius."

17.

Ambrosius journeyed west, to the edge of the storm-wracked shore of Dumnonia. He took thirty men with him for an escort. This was deep inside British territory, his territory, but it paid to be cautious. All kinds of dangers lurked in the forests, besides wild beasts: thieves and runaway slaves, masterless soldiers, wandering bands of sea-raiders, peasants made homeless by the recent wars.

Much like Roman towns and Roman roads, Roman law and order was fast decaying. Nowhere was truly safe, even religious houses.

Ambrosius had cause to reflect on this when he caught sight of the convent. It was a suitably isolated place, built inside a wood near a range of cliffs overlooking the sea, and resembled a miniature fortress, guarded by stone walls and a gatehouse.

The convent itself formed a hollow square, and was built of the same rough grey stone as the outer walls. It had a tiled roof, and the square stump of the bell tower at the western end of the church was visible over the battlements.

Ambrosius had only been here once before, when he delivered his daughter Morgana into the care of the nuns. To help soothe his conscience and calm his wife's fears, he had left a dozen spearmen to guard her.

He composed himself, taking in a deep breath before riding on to the gate.

The abbess was a severe and dried-up old woman, and regarded Ambrosius with scorn.

"You wish to see your daughter," she said, "I cannot prevent you. Indeed, I only wish you came to see her more often. She is a precious creature, touched by God. I cannot imagine why you choose to neglect her."

Ambrosius bridled at her tone. "Do not presume to lecture me," he retorted, "you know nothing of being a parent, or at least I hope you don't. Where is she?"

The abbess pursed her lips, and led him through the open-air cloister in the centre of the complex, towards the dormitory in the south wing.

"Out," she ordered the group of nuns sitting on their narrow beds, talking in low voices, "all save you, Morgana."

Six thin, pale-faced young women in white robes and wimples filed meekly outside, bowing their heads to the abbess and Ambrosius as they passed.

One remained seated on a bed, hands folded in her lap. She was dressed all in white, like the others, and wore a bandage around her eyes.

"Morgana," said the abbess in a much less severe voice, "stand up, girl, and give thanks to God. Your father has come to visit you."

The girl slowly rose to her feet. She had retained a certain grace, her mother's gift, and Ambrosius' heart broke as he looked upon her for the first time in three years.

Morgana lifted her head. "Father," she said, "you will have to come forward. God has taken the last vestige of my sight."

Swallowing, he strode across the bare flagstones and took her hand. Seen up close, she was desperately thin, and her white hand felt as delicate as an autumn leaf.

"Morgana," he said, raising her fingers to his lips and kissing them, "I am sorry for abandoning you. The failure is all mine. I blamed myself for your blindness. God should have punished me for my sins and failures, but chose to punish you instead."

"Punished?" she said, "oh, father, you have little understanding. There is no punishment. God has rewarded me with vision beyond mere sight."

The abbess came forward, uninvited, to join them. "Is it true the holy Germanus once laid his hand upon her?" she asked eagerly, "and blessed her with the bones of saints?"

"Knuckle-bones," Ambrosius replied, irritated by her presence, "he may as well have waved a sheep's skull over her head, for all the good it did. Germanus promised the blessing would restore my daughter's sight within seven days. Nothing happened."

The old woman smiled and wagged her head. "No, no," she said with infuriating condescension, "you were deceived. Through God, the bishop did indeed work a miracle."

She laid a yellow, claw-like hand on Ambrosius' arm. "Your daughter," she added softly, "has the gift of prophecy. Sight beyond sight. She has proved it, time and again."

Ambrosius pulled his arm away. "Prophecy?" he snapped, "what is this nonsense? You make her sound like a witch."

"It is true, father," said Morgana, "I sometimes experience waking dreams. In them I see real people, and events that have yet to come to pass."

"She enters a trance," the abbess explained, "always after prayer. At first she speaks in tongues, the old language of the Hebrews, and gradually switches to Latin. Almost everything she predicts comes true."

"Such as?" asked Ambrosius.

The abbess lifted her hands. "Many things. A bad winter. Failed or successful harvests. Life and death. She predicted the Treachery of the Long Knives, though too late to send out a warning."

The Treachery of the Long Knives, as the massacre organised by Hengist was now called by many, still had the power to send a shudder through Ambrosius. An image flashed through his mind of the last time he saw his father's face, just before the grave-diggers heaped soil over it.

"Your coming here is no surprise to me," said Morgana, "not seven days ago, I experienced another of my visions."

"Prophecies," the abbess corrected her. Morgana meekly ducked her head before continuing.

"The vision concerned the fate of Britannia, our latter-day Israel. And you, I think. Or that is how I interpret it. Sometimes the meaning of the images God sends me are not clear. He tests me, to gauge the strength of my love for Him. Do you wish to hear it?"

No, thought Ambrosius, but felt it would be cruel to say so. Poor, deluded child. Her mind had turned inward, after so many years locked away in this grim convent, and congealed into madness. How he had failed her!

"Go on," he said, readying himself for a tirade of nonsense.

"I saw two dragons," she began, while the abbess looked on in approval, "one was red, the other white. They dwelled under the earth and fought each other for supremacy. Eventually the fury of their combat made the world shake, and caused the hill above them to split. They emerged from the chasm, wreathed in fire and smoke, and fought across the land."

"At first the white dragon was winning, and inflicted terrible wounds on its rival. But gradually the strength of the white dragon faded, while the red grew stronger and stronger. At last the white was utterly defeated and cast into the sea, where it drowned."

"A pretty dream, daughter," said Ambrosius with a wan smile, "and requires little interpretation. The red dragon is a symbol of the Britons, and of me, since I ride under a dragon banner. The white dragon can only represent the Saxons, though your imagery is not quite accurate. They prefer to paint their banners and shields with pictures of boars and stags. Never dragons."

"Nevertheless, it is a hopeful dream, is it not?" said the abbess, "you are destined to win a great victory over the barbarians, and cast them back into the seas from whence they came."

They have concocted this so-called prophecy between them to please me, thought Ambrosius, but realised that could not be. He had sent no advance word of his coming.

"I can stay only one night," he said, "tomorrow I must return to the east, or else the white dragon may eat us all."

That evening the abbess invited Ambrosius and Morgana to dine with her, and the three of them shared a frugal meal in the old woman's private quarters. These were scarcely less comfortless than the rest of the convent, bare stone walls and uncarpeted floors, while the food was plain and served on a bare wooden board.

Ambrosius found conversation difficult. Morgana was a stranger to him – perhaps she always had been – and he couldn't think what to say to her beyond bland pleasantries.

The abbess stepped into the breach. "I was a worldly woman, once," she announced, "late in coming to God."

"Were you married?" Ambrosius asked politely, spooning some of the tasteless fish stew into his mouth.

"Yes. Happily. But then my husband died of a fever, and I was left alone. No children."

"The love of God, my dear," she added, smiling thinly at Morgana, "unlike the love of men, is pure and deathless."

Is that supposed to be comforting? Ambrosius thought angrily. His daughter said nothing. She ate well enough, but there was an essential lack of strength and vitality about her. The terrible thought struck Ambrosius that she may not live long.

He was almost grateful when the abbess spoke again. "What of affairs in the world, lord?" she asked keenly, "we live such quiet, peaceful lives here. The storms in the east hardly touch us."

Ambrosius wiped his mouth before answering. "Vortigern remains in power," he said, "but only because Hengist finds it convenient to keep him alive. He is a mere puppet of the Saxons now. The slave-king, they call him. Londinium is lost. The foederati of the Saxon Shore forts have revolted, and joined their kin in plundering the countryside."

He smiled mirthlessly. "The foederati cast off their allegiance mere days after the Treachery of the Long Knives. It was all planned. Hengist must have been in secret correspondence with them for months."

The abbess looked horror-struck. "Then half the province is overrun!" she cried, raising her hand to her mouth, "can nothing be done? Where are Britannia's armies?"

"The white dragon is in the ascendant," Ambrosius said mildly, "while the red has retreated to the west, to lick its wounds and wait for better days. Britannia is hopelessly divided, Mother Abbess. Hengist killed most of our leaders."

He refrained from telling the worst of it. All through the summer, waves of refugees had poured into the west, bringing with them dire tales of slaughter and destruction. Others, including many nobles and their retinues, had quit Britannia

154

altogether, taking ship to seek exile in Amorica, the country west of Gaul.

Showing impressive co-ordination, the Saxons had broken out of Cent and overwhelmed the eastern half of Maxima Caesariensis. All the major British towns in the east were lost. Camulodunum and Ratae had been overrun, their crumbling walls stormed at night and the scanty garrisons butchered to a man. Most of the citizens had died as well, or been carried off as slaves. Countless smaller towns and villages met with the same fate.

Ambrosius had ridden west, as far as he dared, to witness the chaos for himself. He saw towns laid low by the repeated battering of Saxon rams, and their inhabitants slaughtered. The barbarians showed no mercy. The people – churchmen, priests and secular people alike – were drowned in their own blood. All was glinting swords and crackling flames.

The Saxons had little use for Roman buildings. They tore down the high walls and towers, burned villas and churches after stripping them of treasure, and left behind nothing but fire and corpses and smouldering ruins.

Ambrosius could do nothing to turn back the Saxon advance. He had barely enough men to defend his own territory, and turned back with a heavy heart, unwilling to gaze any longer on the torment of the east.

"I am trying to raise an army," he said, "but my allies are few, and thinly spread. I can at least defend the west, so you may sleep soundly in your beds a while longer."

He spent an uncomfortable night in one of the outbuildings (men were forbidden to sleep inside the convent), and the next morning bade a sad farewell to his daughter.

"I will come and see you again," he promised, "and soon. Or as soon as the war allows."

He kissed Morgana's cold cheek. She didn't respond, so he turned away with a sigh.

"Father," she said with a sudden urgency in her voice, plucking at his sleeve as he was about to climb into the saddle.

"What is it, child?" he asked, smiling fondly at her.

"The prophecy...I did not tell you its full meaning, for fear of offending you."

"Nothing you say could offend me."

"You are wrong. I allowed you to think that you are the red dragon, and would win the final victory over the Saxons. I lied."

She clasped her thin hands together. "I am so sorry, father. The dragon is yet to come. His name shall be exalted, and yours shall be crushed under its weight. This I have seen."

Ambrosius laughed. "I wish him joy, for I have no desire to be exalted. God be with you, my daughter."

He mounted and cantered away, his men streaming after him. Only once did he turn his head and wave at the slender white figure standing under the arch of the gatehouse.

His eyes blurred with tears as he looked at her. The gates slammed shut, and she was gone.

Ambrosius strove to put Morgana out of his mind. His visit to the convent had been an indulgence. One he could ill-afford, with British resistance threatening to collapse in the face of the Saxon advance. As one of the handful of British leaders still alive, his presence was urgently needed at the front, to rally the shattered morale of the survivors.

Morgana was not the only one to suffer prophetic dreams. He had told no-one, not even his wife, but he frequently dreamed of his own death. Death in battle, usually, laid low by a Saxon long-axe. Ambrosius feared it might happen soon, and so decided to visit his daughter while he still could.

Ambrosius thought himself a coward. He was frightened of death, especially of death in battle, of the shrieking agony of hard-forged steel hacking into his flesh. The nightmare of Guoloph had stayed with him over the years. He often remembered the faces of Gwri and Menas, twisted in unspeakable pain as the life was cut from their bodies, and trembled.

Yet, despite his fear, he was resolved to keep fighting until death came for him. If he did not, and failed to give his broken people something to rally around, who would?

AMBROSIUS

He rode east, along a rough track that wound through the deep forest and patches of cultivated land, before meeting with the Roman road. The road followed a typically direct route, linking the town of Isca Dumnoniorum on the south coast with Aquae Sulis and Ratae, before ending at Lindum, far to the north-east. It was in a somewhat dilapidated state, but still useable, and his horsemen made good progress.

He was not heading for Mons Ambrius, but a section of the Roman road some ten miles north-west of the fort. Here the road carved straight through the rolling downs. An enemy host marching from the east would have no alternative but to keep to the road, for the hills flanking it were so steep and thickly wooded as to be virtually impassable.

Ambrosius halted to admire the labours of his workmen. Where the road passed over the flank of a steep-sided combe, rising some six hundred feet above sea level, they had piled up an earthen bank defended by a timber rampart and a dyke on the northern side. The bank cut straight across the road, completely blocking the route from the north-east.

The earthwork continued east and west, and ran for some twelve and a half miles, right across the downs. Originally devised by Ambrosius' father, it had been many years in the planning and construction.

"A linear series of defences," he remembered the old man saying, poring over rough maps of the area, "giving us control over all the roads north of Mons Ambrius."

"Look," Aurelius traced a line across the map with his thumb-nail, "the land is difficult, with plenty of valleys and streams and forests, so first we get our engineers to survey it and mark out the line of the dyke. Then our labourers dig trenches and marker pits at intervals. The pits are dug out and enlarged until they connect, forming the first line of defence. The spare soil is piled up behind the bank, forming the earthwork."

Ambrosius had initially thought it far too ambitious. "We don't have enough men to guard all of it," he said doubtfully.

"Nor do we need them," his father replied, "it won't be like the Wall, with manned forts and watch-towers. All we need to do is control the sections where the dyke crosses the roads. These will be patrolled. The rest of the land is guarded by nature. I can't see Vortigern trying to lead an army through some of those damned forests, can you?"

Ambrosius had continued his father's work, until the dyke now presented a formidable obstacle. Together with Mons Ambrius and the other garrisoned forts to the south, he was able to defend Dumnonia and the roads to the west.

A small camp had sprung up at the foot of the hill, rows of white tents guarded by a palisade, with a long timber barracks-hut in the middle. This was home to the soldiers responsible for guarding the rampart above their heads. A cluster of round wooden huts next to the barracks served to house the labourers and their families.

Ambrosius led his men down to the gate. "We expected you two days ago, lord," said one of the sentries, "you have guests. We lodged them in the barracks."

"Rough comfort," smirked his comrade, "they are doubtless used to softer living."

Ambrosius' brow furrowed. Had Helena come to pay him an unexpected visit? He couldn't blame her for getting bored, shut away on Mons Ambrius.

"I was delayed," he replied curtly, and rode on into the camp.

He dismounted and handed his reins to one of the aides that came running to greet him. As he accepted a flask of wine, the door to the barracks-hut opened and three people emerged.

Two were youngish men, tall and sinewy and well-made. Nobles of some sort, judging from their burnished mail and fur-trimmed cloaks.

Ambrosius failed to recognise them, or their companion, a thin woman with streaks of grey in her chestnut hair. There was a certain facial resemblance between the three, suggesting they were kin.

"Who are you," he demanded, "and why have you sought me out?"

The two young men went down on one knee before him, and the woman bowed her head.

"Lord Ambrosius," she said with dignity, "I am Sevira, once the consort of the High King, now a mere beggar and fugitive. These men who kneel before you are my sons, Vortimer and Catigern."

Ambrosius froze. The ex-wife and two of the three sons of Vortigern, his chief enemy. Delivered into his hands, apparently of their own free will.

His throat was suddenly dry, so he pulled the stopper from the flask and drank. "Why have you come here?" he asked, "you must know I am no friend to Vortigern."

"Nor we, lord king," replied Sevira with a tired but knowing smile, "thanks to him, the Saxons are unleashed. Hengist's filth have seized my crops, slaughtered my servants, and put my houses to the torch. How my father would have wept."

"From the little I know of Magnus Maximus," said Ambrosius, "he would have put aside his tears and looked for revenge."

The elder of the two princes lifted his head. "That is our intention," he growled, "we fled west to offer you our swords. Let us fight by your side, lord, and kill Saxons."

Ambrosius thought quickly. He knew Vortimer and Catigern were estranged from their father, but offering to fight against him was treachery of the blackest sort.

Then again, Vortigern was not the kind of man to inspire loyalty from anyone, even his children.

"How do I know you are who you claim to be?" he said, "Vortigern and Hengist are sly creatures. You may be assassins, sent by them to win my trust and then put a blade in my back."

Sevira paled with anger, but her sons were quick to respond.

"Let us prove ourselves," said the eldest, "send us into battle against the Saxons, and judge us by our deeds."

"We are ready to fight," snarled his brother, "my sword cries out for blood."

Ambrosius wondered how long their enthusiasm would last, in the sweat and cramp and terror of battle. Either they were good liars, or had never seen real fighting before.

He decided to give them an opportunity. Good fighting men were too scarce to be turned away.

"Very well," he said, "you can fight for me in the front line. I shall leave it to God to judge your worth."

18.

All through the following winter Ambrosius waited behind his elaborate ring of defences, preparing for the campaign ahead.

It took time to muster his army. His ally Cunedda sent a hundred Votadinia warriors, all he could spare from the defence of Venedotia. Eidol Cadarn, Ambrosius' other chief ally, sent double that number of light infantry from the garrison of Glevum.

Together with Ambrosius' own men, the comitatenses was almost restored to full strength. He gathered his forces at Mons Ambrius, ready to march east in the spring.

Among the Votadini were two young warriors with familiar faces, or at least they were familiar to Artorius.

"It is always good to meet old friends," he said when he chanced upon them one evening.

With him was Gwalchmei, who had been released from servitude by his master Eidol to train as a soldier. The big, brown-haired boy had swelled into a massive youth, strong as an ox and wide as a barn door. He and Artorius were fast friends.

Cei and Bedwyr looked up from their bowls of bean soup. They were not difficult to recognise. Bigger, stronger, and longer in the limb, they were still the bullies who made Artorius' early childhood a misery. They were about sixteen now, lean and muscular as young warriors should be, dressed in rough woollen cloaks, plaid trousers and sleeveless tunics. Their pale arms were covered from shoulder to wrist in swirling blue tattoos.

Cei was first to speak. "Artúir," he said, brushing soup from his fledgling moustache, "or is it Artorius now? We heard you had put aside your old name."

He chuckled. "Ashamed of your ancestry, eh? I can't blame you. God knows I would be, if I was a Selgovae. Cattle thieves and horse-fuckers, the lot of them."

Artorius smiled away the insults. "You always had a sharp tongue, Cei," he said, "what of you, Bedwyr? Have you any empty noises to make?"

Bedwyr put down his bowl and slowly rose to a crouch. His dark good looks had lived up to their early promise, and he was now a stunningly handsome youth, with limpid blue eyes and curling black hair.

Artorius' hands twitched. It would be pleasant to rob him of his fine looks.

"I seem to remember there was a quarrel between us," he went on in the same light, cheerful tone, "one that was never resolved."

Other men were moving nearer now, drawn by the sound of his voice. Everyone at the fort knew Artorius, who at fourteen was the youngest member of the buccelari, and already one of their best riders.

Oiled steel hissed on leather as he drew his sword. "Get up, the pair of you," he rasped.

To his frustration, they seemed reluctant to fight. "You are Ambrosius' adopted son," said Cei, "heir to the Dux Bellorum. If we hurt you, your father will have us flayed alive."

"Don't worry, lads," said Gwalchmei, "you won't touch him without getting through me first."

Artorius gestured at his friend to stand aside. "This is my fight," he said firmly, "the red-headed swine once kicked my dog. He is mine to chastise."

This was too much for Cei, who uttered a wordless roar and threw himself at Artorius. His sword flashed bright in his hand.

There was fearsome strength in Cei's brawny shoulders and big, clutching hands, but he was slow. Artorius dodged his wild charge and slashed at his head. He used the flat of the blade, intending only to hurt his old tormentors, not kill them.

Cei managed to knock aside the blow, but was thrown off-balance. Their swords locked as Artorius closed, hooked his foot behind Cei's right ankle, and butted him in the chest.

The bigger youth was thrown onto his back. Howling in rage, he would have sprang back up, but Gwalchmei seized him by the neck.

"You're beaten, friend," he said, "accept it, and stay down."

AMBROSIUS

In response Cei's fist swung round and smashed into Gwalchmei's cheek. The two went down, rolling in the dirt and clawing at each other like wild dogs, while Artorius turned to deal with Bedwyr.

He was more circumspect than Cei, and had a better grip on his temper. His handsome face was a mask of concentration as he blocked and parried Artorius' furious blows, all the while giving ground, offering no attacks of his own.

"Trying to wear me out, eh?" panted Artorius, grinning through a film of sweat, "clever, but I'm not going to chase you around like a wild dog."

He halted and planted his legs wide, beckoning at his opponent to come at him. There was a ring of bodies around them now, harsh male voices raised in excitement, roaring him on. One or two – Votadini, no doubt – cheered for Cei and Bedwyr.

Bedwyr straightened up from his fighting stance and dropped his sword. "This is foolish," he said, folding his arms, "if I offended you when we were children, I apologise."

Groans broke out among the crowd. They wanted to see blood. A few voices shouted "Coward!" at Bedwyr, but he ignored them.

Artorius snorted. *Bedwyr makes me look petty*, he thought, *what kind of man nurses a grudge over bruises he suffered as a child?*

Since he had apologised, and thrown down his sword, Artorius could not strike him without being seen as dishonourable. Even so, it was tempting to step forward and give him one ringing, open-handed slap across the face, in payment for all the blows Artorius had taken from him.

Artorius never got to decide. The ground shook under the thunder of hoofs, and the crowd hurriedly parted to let five riders through.

They were led by Ambrosius, whose usual composure had deserted him. "What in God's name is this?" he shouted, his face scarlet as he took in the scene, "brawling in camp? I'll not have it!"

Cei and Gwalchmei were still grovelling in the dirt, throwing punches and curses at each other. They didn't seem to hear Ambrosius, so four men stepped out of the crowd and pulled them apart. Judging from the bruises on each boy's face, and the blood leaking from their mouths and noses, the honours were about even.

Artorius stepped forward. "No brawl, father," he said, sheathing his sword, "merely a little friendly sparring that got out of hand."

Ambrosius glared down at him. "I expected better of you," he said quietly, recovering some of his poise, "and you should know better than to lie to me."

"Father, I..." Artorius began, but Ambrosius raised his hand for silence.

"Enough. You have not only encouraged a breach of discipline, but taken an active role in it. Shamed, in front of the soldiers you will lead one day."

Their eyes met. Artorius was fond of his adoptive father, but realised he had underestimated him. There was steel under the Roman's gentle, patient demeanour, and now it was drawn.

He means to teach me a lesson. For my own good.

"I believe we have met before," said Ambrosius, turning to Cei and Bedwyr, "years ago, at Curia, I told you what the penalty for assaulting a comrade was. Do you remember?"

Cei glowered in silence, wiping the blood from his lip, but Bedwyr answered smartly. "Twenty lashes with a vine rod, sir," he said.

"Correct. It was meant as a warning, one you and your friend have failed to heed. A reminder is in order."

"Decurio," he said, turning his head to address the officer behind him, "three of these men are to be flogged. They are young, so the sentence is commuted to ten lashes each."

Ambrosius' eyes were full of anger and disappointment as they looked down at Artorius. "Not this one," he added, "he can watch, and help salve their wounds afterwards."

The sentence was carried out, and Artorius made to play his part. Before the eyes of the assembled troops on the plain outside

164

the fort, Cei, Bedwyr and Gwalchmei were tied to stakes and flogged until their backs ran with blood.

When the punishment was over, they were untied and carried up to the hall, where Artorius helped the slaves to wash away the blood with wine and rub liniment into the livid cuts.

Gwalchmei was the first to revive from his swoon. "Army discipline," he mumbled, his face pressed to the board, "I hoped never to taste it. Thank God my mother can't see me."

"I'm sorry," said Artorius, and meant it. "I will repay the debt. To all of you."

While the boys recovered, Ambrosius made his final preparations for the campaign. He worked fast, and the chill of late winter was still in the air when his army moved out in force, following the most direct route to Londinium.

Artorius, suitably chastened by his recent humiliation, rode just behind the dragon banner. Once they were fit enough to ride, Cei and Bedwyr were among the Votadini horsemen Ambrosius sent ahead as scouts.

Gwalchmei rode beside Artorius. The flogging had done little to sour his naturally easy-going disposition, and he held no grudges.

"We deserved it," he said, wincing at every jolt and bit of rough ground his horse went over, "and got off lightly, really. The legions of old used to execute men for brawling."

"I should have taken the flogging," said Artorius, "thirty lashes, all on my own back."

Gwalchmei glanced sidelong at him. "That's easy to say now," he remarked, "and Ambrosius would have refused anyway. He is grooming you to succeed him as Dux Bellorum. He wanted you to feel guilt, not the sting of the rod."

"I know," snapped Artorius, "I'm not stupid."

He looked ahead, to the distant banners of the Votadini, about a mile ahead of the main army. Cei and Bedwyr were insolent dogs, but he needed to win their loyalty. Their friendship, even. One day they would fight for him. No leader could afford to harbour enemies in his own ranks.

Artorius continued to brood on his mistakes as the army pushed on, meeting with no opposition. The land east of Mons Ambrius was stripped of human life, the native population having fled the onslaught of the Saxons, deserting their farms and villages.

Artorius witnessed some of the ravages of war: the blackened, burned-out shells of houses and farmsteads and the rotting corpses of their inhabitants lying scattered outside, like so many dead birds.

"They have lain there for months," remarked Gwalchmei, "since last autumn, probably, with no-one to bury them. Look, you can see the bones poking through their flesh."

Artorius forced himself to look. One in his position, fated to lead men in battle, could not afford to be squeamish.

The Saxons had scoured the land of anything valuable, scarcely leaving a pot or a stray chicken behind. Doubtless they had taken plenty of slaves as well, killing those who tried to resist or were deemed unfit to serve.

My own people are no different, he reflected, *had my father lived, and the attack on our village never happened, I might even now be leading raids on our neighbours, stealing cattle and pigs and cutting the throats of defenceless peasants.*

Ambrosius advanced cautiously, wary of sudden ambushes. Artorius thought he meant to lay siege to Londinium, but instead the army swung south-east, towards the Saxon territory of Cent. He sent out more scouts, covering the flanks of his army as well as the vanguard, with orders to return as soon as they caught a glimpse of the enemy.

Much of the land in this part of the country was cultivated, the ancient forests that once covered the whole of Britannia long since cleared away. Artorius thought Vortigern must have been mad to give it away so cheaply to barbarians.

Three more days passed, and still there was no sign of the Saxons. "They knew we were coming, and retreated," Gwalchmei said confidently, "they won't face cavalry in open battle."

At last the army reached a belt of dense woodland, stretching away for miles to the south. Artorius knew this was the edge of a great swathe of forest that cut off the coastal plain from the rest of Britannia.

Ambrosius halted the main part of his army in the desolate fields a mile from the forest, and sent a few of the Votadini ahead to explore.

They swiftly returned, streaming out of the trees as though all the hounds of Hell were at their heels.

"Saxons!" Artorius heard Bedwyr shout, his swarthy features flushed with excitement, "they are in the woods!" "Hundreds of them," Cei added breathlessly, "drawn up in long lines among the trees. We saw a white-haired giant among them. They threw spears at us, but all their warriors are on foot. We got away easily."

Ambrosius summoned a council of war. "The white-haired giant can only be Horsa," he said, "he wants to draw us into the forest, where his axes can cut down our horsemen at will. I don't mean to oblige him."

He gazed to the east. Artorius thought he looked more lean and severe than ever. Ambrosius was in his forties now. He had led a tough life, full of sorrow and loss, and it had aged him. There were touches of grey at his temples, and deep lines carved into his thin face. His shoulders were slightly hunched, as though it was an effort to hold himself upright.

"The infantry will have to clear them out," he murmured, rubbing his jaw, "it will be hard and bloody work. We will lose many men. The Saxons don't like to yield ground easily."

Ambrosius smiled bleakly at the little group of officers. "Do I have any volunteers to lead the assault?" he asked.

"Not you," he added sharply as Artorius started forward, "your courage is admirable, but I won't risk losing my son and heir to some chance blow in a skirmish. You fight only when you have to."

Artorius stepped back, disappointed, and two other men eagerly took his place. He regarded them with a mixture of jealousy and distrust. They claimed to be Vortimer and Catigern, two of the High King's three sons, recently fled from the chaos in the east to offer their swords to the British resistance.

"Give us command of the infantry, lord," begged the eldest, "let us prove our worth, as you promised."

Ambrosius looked doubtful. "Neither of you have any real experience of war," he said, "this battle will be no place for novices or faint hearts. The Saxons will fight like hellcats."

"We will drive them from the forest," Catigern replied stoutly, "or die."

Ambrosius thought for a moment, pulling at his slightly misshapen nose, broken in an ancient skirmish. "Very well," he said eventually, "tomorrow morning, just before dawn, you will have your opportunity. Until then, get as much rest as possible."

"Why wait until tomorrow morning?" Artorius asked later, after the council had broken up, "what if the Saxons slip away during the night?"

Ambrosius was sitting on the ground, gnawing at a strip of dried meat. "If they abandon their position, so much the better," he replied with a shrug, "but I don't think they will. They cannot retreat forever. No, the Saxons will try and stop us in the forest, where our cavalry cannot get at them."

"As to the timing," he continued, "men are at their weakest in the cold grey hours just before sunrise, especially if they have been deprived of sleep. With luck, Horsa will keep his warriors up all night, waiting for us to attack. Meanwhile, our men shall have rested."

He squinted at the dark line of forest. "It will be a near thing. God help us."

Artorius again reflected on the deceptive ruthlessness of the man seated before him. Ambrosius knew he was sending his soldiers to die, and yet did so anyway. What else could he do? The only other option was to give up the war as lost and slink back to the west, leaving a huge swathe of British territory in Saxon hands.

The Britons settled down to wait. Artorius sought out Gwalchmei, and the pair shared their rations.

Artorius was finishing off his meagre portion of bacon when a shadow fell across him.

"For God's sake," he sighed, glancing up at Cei and Bedwyr, "can we not leave aside our quarrel, at least until the battle is over?"

"We've not come to fight," said Bedwyr, "but to make peace. None of us may see another nightfall. A man's soul should be free of hatred before it goes to meet God."

He knelt and stuck out his right hand. After some hesitation, Artorius clasped it.

"Now you, Cei," said Bedwyr, without looking up at his friend. Cei glowered, but eventually knelt to offer his hand as well.

They repeated the ceremony with Gwalchmei. "Now we're all friends," he said affably, "why not sit down and have some of our ale? It's foul muck, but might help you sleep."

"We're not friends," snarled Cei, rising quickly, "just comrades. There is a difference."

He hurried back to the campfire where the Votadini sat. Bedwyr rolled his eyes and jogged after him.

"Well, that's something," remarked Gwalchmei, "they may not love us, but they won't slit our throats in the night either."

"Plenty of time for throat-slitting," said Artorius, gazing nervously to the east. The late afternoon light was starting to darken, and he could hear the faint rumble of drums from inside the forest.

"The Saxons will keep that hellish din going all night. They want to frighten us."

Gwalchmei lay back on the grass and folded his hands behind his head. "If the fools want to tire their arms out, let them," he replied carelessly, "come the dawn, they will have no strength left."

Artorius got little sleep. The drums kept him awake, along with Gwalchmei's thunderous snoring. His mind was restless, and kept mulling over ways of driving the Saxons from their den without sacrificing so many British lives.

A flanking manoeuvre, perhaps, he thought, *small bands of chosen men sent to work their way around the fringes of the Saxon host.*

It wouldn't do. Artorius had little idea of how many Saxons were in the forest – hundreds, according to the Votadini, which wasn't much help – or how they were deployed. There was no room for subtle tactics here. The issue would to be settled, one way or the other, by a head-on assault.

In the cold grey light of dawn, the Britons attacked. They advanced in silence, preceded by no bugles or war-horns.

Artorius watched the mass of the infantry, organised in a single phalanx, move towards the trees. Vortimer and Catigern jogged a few paces ahead of the front line. Both wore helmets and knee-length mail shirts, and the blades of their spathas shone in the gloom.

The drums stopped. A brief silence followed, broken by a roar as the Britons stormed forward.

Artorius' later memories of that terrible morning were confused. The fighting lasted until well after sunrise, and he remembered a constant flow of wounded and crippled men limping out of the woods, or else carried by their comrades; the rows of blankets spread out by the British medical orderlies on the ground, and the bleeding, ruined bodies laid out on them; the screams and moans of the dying, the noise of battle, clashing steel mingled with voices raised in pain and fury, triumph and despair; Ambrosius, his face white with strain, tearing strips from his purple cloak when the bandages started to run out, and handing them to the orderlies.

Above all he remembered a hoarse voice singing softly as its owner slowly bled his life out.

"It is not the spear that pierces me with pain,
From the beginning of the end until midnight,
I will keep awake, I will weep with the dawn,
It is not my death that scares me,
On this red dawn, and causes my heart to slow,
And the red tears to flow,
It is not the shadow of death that torments me,
In this ending, this final hour, my feeble passing,
But my brothers and my country I mourn…"

170

AMBROSIUS

Five times the British infantry were thrown back, leaving their dead and wounded strewn among the trees, where the Saxons cut their throats and pillaged the bodies.

Enraged by this violation of their slain comrades, the British rallied and went in again. Vortimer and Catigern were at the forefront of every charge, their blades wet to the hilt with Saxon blood, fearless in their battle-fury, like heroes from some ancient poem.

The casualties continued to trickle out of the forest, but after the fifth assault they returned in the grip of a strange euphoria, grinning and laughing in spite of their wounds.

"We've beaten them," Artorius overhead one man crow, supporting a smaller comrade whose right leg had been axed off at the knee, "that last charge broke the shieldwall."

"The bastards are running," cried another, barely more than a boy, blood and teeth spitting from a hideous gash in his cheek, "running like hares."

Their joy was infectious, and a mood of jubilation swept through the army, even while the exhausted, sweating orderlies laboured to save the lives of the broken men on the blankets.

Ambrosius remained tense and silent, until the dawn mist had fully risen and the last of the British survivors had returned from the woods.

Vortimer was among them, all his fury spent, walking like a man in a dream. His helmet was dinted, his mail spattered with blood, and he carried a Saxon long-axe in place of his sword.

"Well fought, my prince," said Ambrosius, "I doubt you no more. No veteran could have done better."

Under the smears of blood and dirt, the young man's face was haggard, and looked to have aged some thirty years in a single morning.

"My brother is dead," he said in a hollow voice, "he met Horsa in single combat. I tried to reach them in time, but failed. Horsa cut off his sword-arm, and then his head. His body lies in the forest."

"Catigern was always brave. Even when we were boys, he dreamed of performing some heroic feat of arms. He wanted his name to live forever in song."

"So it will," Ambrosius said gently, "you and Catigern broke the shieldwall. Thanks to your courage, we have won a great victory."

Artorius saw the red spark of anger in Vortimer's eyes, and heard the savagery in his tired voice.

"No victory," he growled, tightening his grip on the axe, "there can be no victory, until I see Horsa lying dead at my feet."

19.

Scorching afternoon sunlight beat down on the faces of the Saxon host as they stood on the eastern bank of the ford, and waited.

They were battered, war-weary, scarred and hurting from their defeat in the forest. Two days had passed since the battle, during which time Hengist and Horsa worked frantically to rally the survivors and make them ready to fight again.

My people have never lacked for courage, Hengist thought proudly as he ran a critical eye over his warriors. He and his brother had managed to pull together some three hundred men. The rest were dead or scattered.

Three hundred warriors, formed up into a shieldwall to defend this river crossing, a few miles south of the town of Durobrivae. If the Britons won here, they would break through into the very heart of Cent, the territory Hengist had taken from Vortigern as his sister's bride-price.

Cent was a paradise of rich soil and verdant countryside, with the salt tang of the sea never far away. From the moment he set foot on British soil, Hengist had wanted it for himself. Any man would be glad to die to defend such a land.

Hengist had little intention of dying. He was no coward, but considered his skin too precious to risk in battle unless absolutely necessary. What would his people be, without him to lead them? Just another wandering tribe, with no greater destiny in mind than piracy and feuding.

He stood behind the shieldwall, guarded by six gesiths. East of the river, the ground rose sharply, and he was able to see over the heads of his warriors.

His brother Horsa, as always, stood in the middle of the front line, under his V-shaped boar standard. The ageing giant was a totem in himself, a pillar of the Saxon race, and his massive, brooding presence put fresh heart into the men around him. Some of the more credulous warriors were beginning to speak of him as a god, the living embodiment of Geta, one of their rough pagan deities.

Horsa had distinguished himself in the battle in the forest, slaying a British prince in single combat. The death of the prince had sent a shudder through the British warriors, but not enough to make them turn and flee.

Hengist heard the sound of trumpets, and spied the first of the dragon standards advancing over the horizon. The British infantry advanced in five orderly divisions of spearmen, flanked by slingers and archers. Their superior numbers had carried the day in the forest, and they still outnumbered the Saxons almost two to one.

After them came the dreaded cavalry. Hengist strained his eyes to make out the figure of Ambrosius, distinctive in his purple cloak and crested helmet, trotting at the head of a small troop of personal guards.

"My last enemy," muttered Hengist. Now most of the other British leaders were dead, slaughtered in the Treachery of the Long Knives, effective command of native resistance had passed to Ambrosius. Once he was removed, little would stand between the Saxons and conquest of the British mainland.

This was the second time in two days Hengist had laid eyes on him. Prior to that, he had never seen Ambrosius before, but learned to respect his abilities from afar. Only one with a sound grasp of strategy and organisation could have overseen the construction of the mighty network of defences in the west. Only an inspirational leader could have rallied his forces after Guoloph, and forged a new army from the tattered rags of the old.

Ambrosius would do nothing hasty, Hengist knew. He would halt and rest his men, and take careful stock of the Saxon defences before ordering an assault.

This time, he would be sending them into a trap. Hengist's men were spread thin, covering all the open ground east of the crossing. Their flanks were guarded by dense woodland.

Hengist had ordered a double row of stakes, hastily cut from the woods, to be plunged into the shallow mud of the river immediately in front of the Saxon position. These presented the Britons with a fearsome obstacle. The stakes would break up the momentum of the British assault, demoralising and impeding their men even before they faced the Saxon axes.

As the enemy marched closer, the Saxons started beating on their shields and yelling war-cries – *"Ut, ut! (out, out!)"* and *"Hund! (cowards!)"*

The Britons were largely silent, though a few of the more devout soldiers chanted psalms and called on God.

As Hengist had predicted, their infantry halted on the edge of the river. Barely half a bow-shot separated the armies, close enough for the warriors on both sides to make out the faces of those they meant to kill.

The crossing was no more than thigh-deep, and wide enough for a dozen men to wade abreast. Ambrosius would have to attack on this narrow front, hoping his spearmen could punch a hole in the shieldwall while his archers and slingers rained missiles down on Saxon heads.

Hengist's warriors would simply have to endure the storm. Man for man, they were more than a match for the Britons in close combat. They had homes and families to defend, a land to fight for, and the presence of Horsa to encourage them. With luck, and the favour of their gods, these would prove enough.

Ambrosius' archers poured into the gaps between the compact squares of infantry. The Saxon war-cries faded as they raised their shields high to guard against the inevitable hail of arrows.

Hengist help up his own shield, made from a round piece of linden wood covered on both sides by pieces of cow-hide. He heard the British captains give the order to loose, and tensed, waiting for the impact.

There was a brief pause, and then a sound like the thudding of hammers on wood as the arrows fell. One of Hengist's gesiths howled and dropped his shield, cursing as he hopped about with a green-fletched arrow sticking from his left foot.

Screams and curses erupted from the Saxon ranks, mixed with the occasional gurgle as an arrow found an exposed throat, but there were few casualties. The Saxons were well-protected by their shields, helmets and leather and mail byrnies, and would not be forced from the field so easily.

More arrows fell, mixed with stones from the British slingers who had waded into the shallows. The missiles pattered like rain off the overlapping wall of Saxon shields.

Hengist was confident. Soon Ambrosius would realise the futility of trying to win the battle at long range, and send his infantry splashing across the river. Then the real killing would begin.

It all unfolded as he hoped. The storm of missiles died away, a peal of bugles cut through the heavy air, and the British spears advanced.

"Make ready!" Hengist heard his brother roar. The Saxons in the front rank lowered their shields and drew back their angons, ready to throw. Both sides would exchange showers of javelins before closing.

The British ranks disintegrated as they waded through the muddy water and found a nasty surprise waiting for them: Hengist had ordered the lower ends of the stakes to be roped together. Hidden underwater, the ropes caused many of the unwary Britons to trip and stumble.

"Loose!" Horsa bellowed, and his Saxons hurled their angons into the mass of enemy warriors.

Hengist felt a thrill of pleasure at the sound of British screams, and the sight of their soldiers floundering and dying in the river. Their blood tainted the churning brown waters, turning it a deep shade of crimson.

The British square dissolved into chaos, officers bawling in vain at their men to close up and hurl their javelins. Angons and throwing axes carved bloody holes in their disordered ranks. Only the bravest or luckiest survived the missile storm and fought their way through the fence of stakes.

Horsa lumbered into the water and swung his long-axe at a British officer. The Briton tried to get his sword up in time to stave off the blow, but the glittering blade cut through his wrist and shoulder, chopping through his mail like butter and cleaving him to the groin. More blood and entrails stained the water as his body fell apart in two ragged halves.

The Saxons roared their admiration of Horsa's latest heroic exploit. He turned to acknowledge their cheers, shaking his bloody axe above his head.

Hengist's single eye widened as he saw another British officer charging in to avenge his comrade. He recognised this man, one of the two who had led the British so fearlessly in the forest. Horsa had slain the other.

"Horsa!" he shouted, but he was too far away, his voice lost among the tumult.

The officer hurled his javelin. Just six feet from Horsa, he could scarcely miss. The slender dart found a gap in the giant's ring-mail and stuck into the small of his massive back.

Hengist knew his brother was almost impervious to pain. At Guoloph, he had fought on with terrific savagery despite suffering countless wounds, eventually collapsing through sheer loss of blood. A javelin in the back might be enough to fell most men, but to Horsa would be a mere pin-prick.

Even a pin-prick was enough to rouse his awesome temper. Bellowing with rage, he swung around, striking blindly with his axe. The Briton ducked under the wild flash of steel, ripped out his spatha and charged forward, hacking at Horsa's legs.

The steel cut deep into the flesh below Horsa's knee. He staggered and almost fell, gaping in shock at the bright red blood gushing from the wound. Used to intimidating opponents, he seemed taken off-guard by the Briton's ferocity.

Stranded behind the shieldwall, Hengist could only watch the duel play itself out. Leaning awkwardly on his good leg, Horsa swung again and again at the Briton, who danced around him like an insect taunting a bear, stabbing and hacking. The din of battle ebbed as the eyes of both sides were drawn to the combat.

"God aid Vortimer!" Hengist overheard some of the Britons shout, and his suspicions were confirmed. The man fighting his brother was the High King's eldest son.

He ground his teeth. When this war was over, he would murder Vortigern with his own hands. The old man had expended his usefulness. Rowena might protest – she had conceived a strange affection for her husband – but he would soon find her a new mate. A good Saxon this time, who would give her the sons Vortigern's decrepit seed had failed to deliver.

Soon the British prince's sword was red to the hilt. Gasping for breath, sweat mingling with the blood flowing from a gash above his right eye, Horsa slowly crumpled to his knees.

His armour had protected him from the worst of Vortimer's blows, but his face and hands and legs were awash with blood. Three fingers had been sheared from his left hand, and he could no longer wield his axe properly.

A ragged cheer broke from the watching Britons as Vortimer tugged off Horsa's battered helmet, tossed it aside and grasped a handful of the Saxon's long white hair. Then he threw aside his spatha and drew his dagger.

"Catigern!" he yelled, yanking back Vortimer's head to slash his throat.

At the same time Horsa's long arms swept upwards, and his remaining fingers wrapped round Vortimer's neck. They squeezed like a vice, choking the breath out of him.

Vortimer panicked and stabbed wildly at the ruin of Horsa's face. His blade opened fresh wounds, but still he was dragged down, into the water. Horsa held him there, his huge hands pushing Vortimer's head under, ignoring the waves of silt and blood-flecked mud kicked up by his opponent's thrashing limbs.

After a final spasm Vortimer lay still, and a groan of dismay rose from British throats. The cry of triumph from the Saxons was checked as Horsa's eyes closed. Fresh blood bubbled up from the water above his groin.

"No," Hengist whispered as the giant slowly toppled forward to lie on top of Vortimer's corpse.

Horsa wallowed for a second or two, like a dying whale, and turned over onto his back. All could see the hilt of the dagger protruding from his crotch. Even as he drowned, Vortimer had struck a fatal blow, stabbing upwards, under the skirts of Horsa's mail.

The passing of the two champions stunned both armies into silence. Hengist frenziedly pushed and shoved his way through the ranks of the shieldwall, his gesiths hard on his heels.

"Out of the way, you scum," he shouted, battering men aside with his shield and the flat of his sword, "move aside – move, if you value your hides!"

He broke free of them and stumbled into the river.

"Horsa," he sobbed, kneeling in the water beside the bleeding hulk of his brother, "speak, Horsa. Live. Breathe. You cannot go before me."

Horsa was silent, his lips peeled back to reveal the blackish stumps of his teeth, eyes staring at nothing. Retching with grief and shock, Hengist draped his cloak over the dead man's head and shoulders.

"Help me!" he screamed at his gesiths, "help me lift him!"

Between them they managed to heave Horsa's dead weight onto their shoulders. Even as the Saxons carried Horsa to the shore, staggering under his bulk, a group of British spearmen plucked Vortimer's body from the river.

There was no more fighting that day. Neither side had any stomach for it. The Britons withdrew, taking their dead with them, to make camp for the night on the plains to the west.

The Saxons were left in possession of the ford, but there was no jubilation among them.

"Better a thousand of our warriors should die, than you," Hengist murmured brokenly as he sat beside the corpse of his brother, "better all our ships should burn, all our lands vanish below the waves, all our women and gold and slaves be delivered into the hands of Christian men."

How he had despised his brother in life, thinking him nothing but a tool, a useful killer. Too late, he now realised what Horsa had meant to him. They were joined in blood and soul. Born into the dreary flatlands of northern Germania, a world of squalid blood-feuds and tribal squabbling, they had dreamed of a greater future for their people, and crossed an ocean together to achieve it. They had made a king tremble, and come within a sword's edge of realising their dream.

The gods were as fickle as they were cruel. They had ripped Horsa's soul from his body and cast it into shadow, to await his brother in the halls of the dead. Hengist was left to fight on, as though any man could fight without his sword-arm.

There was a full moon that night. Shafts of pale light shone down on Horsa's body, surrounding it with an unearthly glow. Hengist remained lost in grief for hours, deaf to the sound of his warriors moving in respectful silence around him.

At last one of his gesiths worked up the courage to speak. "Lord," he said, kneeling beside his chief, "what are we to do? If we stay here, the Britons will attack again in the morning."

He lowered his voice to a confidential whisper. "I've looked at the men, lord, and I don't think they can fight again. Not so soon. The death of Horsa has taken something out of them."

Horsa bit back his first response, which was to tell the man to crawl away and die in a hole, and tried to think. He was the chief now, the leader and the ring-giver, and the fate of his people depended entirely on him. It always had done, of course, but he could no longer hide behind Horsa's gigantic shadow.

"We will retreat," he replied, "march away during the night, and take refuge on the Isle of Tanatos."

The Isle of Tanatos lay off the eastern coast of Cent, divided from the mainland by a river which could be crossed on foot at low tide. Hengist had ordered a fort to be built on its summit, a last refuge in case his people ever needed one.

"Are you certain, lord?" the gesith asked, "it means abandoning Cent to the enemy."

Hengist made a great effort to cling onto his temper. "I know, you oaf," he hissed, "but if the men won't fight, then they must run. Otherwise Ambrosius will slay us all."

"Order them to break camp," he added in a firmer voice, averting his eyes from Horsa's corpse, "we move out immediately."

20.

Ambrosius rode past the charred remains of crops in the fields, empty farmsteads, and the corpses of slaves and freemen who had foolishly tried to defend their mistress's property. The reward for such loyalty was death, and the winners lay rotting by the roadside.

Later, if he remembered, Ambrosius would send men to give the dead Christian burial. The crops would be re-sown, farmsteads rebuilt. Slowly, the marks of the Saxon revolt would vanish from the face of the land, leaving Britannia whole again.

Not quite whole, he reminded himself bitterly, *the plague of Saxons cannot be wholly eradicated.*

Thanks to the treachery of the foederati garrison troops, the barbarians still had their claws dug into the eastern seaboard of Britannia. Most of the Saxon Shore forts were firmly in enemy hands, along with the strip of coastline they controlled.

Using the forts as a base, Saxon war-bands were probing inland, taking over deserted British villages and farms, squatting in the ruins of larger towns such as Camulodunum.

Ambrosius didn't have the men to drive them out. Most of his forces were still in Cent, laying siege to the Isle of Tanatos, where Hengist had retreated with the remnant of his followers. If Britannia still had a navy (Vortigern had never bothered with the expense of maintaining one) they might have attacked and sunk Hengist's ships, stranding him and his men on the island. As it was, the Saxons might have easily escaped if they wished, but Hengist seemed reluctant to give up his last piece of British territory.

The siege had been dragging on for weeks. Ambrosius chose to leave the conduct of it in the hands of capable officers and ride north, skirting Londinium, to visit the country estates of Sevira, Vortigern's former wife.

Sevira had returned to her family home, to try and salvage something from the ruin. After the deaths of her sons in battle,

Ambrosius had sent her their bodies, respectfully wrapped in purple cloaks with their swords and helmets laid by their sides.

They were carried back to their mother in a covered wagon, with a priest to pray for their souls and a strong mounted escort to guard against bandits or wandering bands of Saxons, hungry for revenge.

Ambrosius thought the purple cloaks a nice touch, considering their ancestry, and hoped Sevira would have got over the worst of her grief by the time he arrived. He had enough death and sorrow to cope with. Hundreds of his soldiers had died in the recent fighting, and provision needed to be made for their wives and children.

Sevira's house was one of the largest still-occupied villas in Britannia, a huge complex of private dwellings and outbuildings, built of white dressed stone and roofed with red tiles.

The gates to the living quarters and the fermenting yard had been smashed in, as had the costly tinted glass in all the windows. Ambrosius shuddered to think of the devastation inside. He pictured Saxon warriors rampaging from room to room, their faces streaked with soot, axes dripping with the blood of murdered slaves. Incapable of appreciating the beauty and refinements of civilisation, they would have defaced the frescoes, smashed the furnishings, torn down the tapestries and wall-hangings and got swine-drunk on the contents of the wine cellar.

He stopped about half a mile from the villa, which stood in the middle of some fifty acres of flat, cultivated land.

"Decurio," he said, "ride to the house, and wait for me outside. I shan't be long."

"Yes, sir," replied the officer, and signalled at the men, twenty buccelari Ambrosius had brought for an escort, to follow him.

Meanwhile Ambrosius rode north-west, towards the church standing beside a stream that ran in a more or less straight line through the fields, before vanishing into the woods.

The church was built of the same white stone as the villa. It was a square, compact building, with three narrow arched windows above the door and a peaked roof. Ambrosius had spotted a familiar figure standing in the doorway.

Sevira was bareheaded, and wore a dark blue wide-sleeved tunic called a dalmatic. Ambrosius reined in sharply when another figure stepped out of the darkness of the church to stand beside her. This was a young man, a few inches taller than Sevira, bright mail gleaming under his cloak.

Ambrosius forced himself to relax a little. The young man carried no weapons that he could see.

Nor did the Saxons when they murdered your father.

Determined to be on his guard, he urged his horse a little closer. His eyes narrowed. The windows above the door were dark and empty, but might easily hide an archer.

Sevira spoke first. "Lord Ambrosius," she called out, "I thought it best to greet you here. My house is in a lamentable state. A handful of loyal slaves remain in my service, and they are doing their best to tidy up the damage, but it won't be fit to receive guests until the autumn."

She spoke courteously, but Ambrosius recognised the marks of sorrow and bereavement on her face. Sevira's eyes her eyes had a dull, listless quality, as though weary of gazing upon the world and its horrors. He noticed the young man lay his hand on her shoulder, an oddly protective gesture.

"My lady," he said, "never fear, I did not come to impose upon your hospitality. Who is this?"

"My youngest son, Pascent," she replied, "my only living son now. The others lie inside the church. Resting for all time in the family vault, lapped in stone and lead."

"Thank you for sending them to me," she added gravely.

"Lord," said Pascent, bowing. Ambrosius ran a critical eye over him. Unlike his late brothers, he bore little physical resemblance to Sevira. His stocky build, muddy brown hair and dark colouring were all his father's gifts.

"The Saxons were keeping you as a hostage," said Ambrosius, "along with your father in Londinium. Did they release you?"

"Not exactly, lord," Pascent answered, "when word of the death of Horsa and the flight of Hengist reached the city, most of the Saxon garrison deserted and fled to their ships. They thought your army would soon be at the gates. Myself and the other captives were left unguarded, free to depart."

Ambrosius had planned to leave Londinium until Hengist was defeated, preferring not to waste his limited strength laying siege to the most well-defended city in Britannia. The news that the Saxons had simply abandoned the place was heartening, but he was eager to know of the High King's whereabouts.

"What of your father?" he asked, "did he flee with the Saxons?"

"No, lord. I last saw him riding in the direction of Verulamium with all the loyal followers he could gather. No more than a dozen men. He took Rowena with him as well."

Ambrosius spat. "I find it difficult to believe that your father could find even a dozen men willing to serve him," he said coldly, "he sacrificed the loyalty of every one of his subjects, save the barbarian filth he invited in to destroy us."

And you, he added silently as Pascent looked embarrassed and hung his head, *Vortimer and Catigern broke with their father, but you did not.*

Such loyalty, even if misplaced, should not be wasted. Perhaps I can find a use for Pascent.

He put aside the thought for now. "So the tyrant has fled," he went on, "where might he have gone? The foederati in the east might receive him, though God knows he is worth little to them now."

"No," said Sevira before her son could respond, "he has run to the west, to beg for sanctuary from his own people."

Her voice oozed with hatred for her one-time husband. "Ride west, Ambrosius, and you will find him skulking behind the walls of Viroconium. Unless even the Cornovii reject him. If so, you might find him anywhere. A landless, rootless, homeless beggar, wandering the wilds of Britannia, despised and shunned by all right-thinking folk."

You would rejoice to see that come to pass, my lady, thought Ambrosius, *perhaps we could serve up his head on a platter to you, as Salome demanded the head of John the Baptist.*

He found Sevira's tone distasteful, but could hardly blame her. Nor did he intend to be any less unmerciful. It was time to put an end to Vortigern.

"Father will seek refuge in Powys," said Pascent, "he told me so, before he left Londinium." Ambrosius stared hard at him, trying to divine some hidden motive behind his words. Pascent's face was open and guileless, almost foolish in its lack of cunning.

"Why did you not go with him?" he asked.

Pascent laid an arm around Sevira's shoulders. "I heard of the passing of Vortimer and Catigern," he replied defensively, "and wished to be with my mother. I am all she has left."

Was there an accusing note in his voice? If so, it was quickly smothered.

"Your brothers fought and died like heroes," said Ambrosius, "they broke the shieldwall, and brought down Horsa. Without their sacrifice, this war would still be in the balance."

Sevira's eyes lost something of their tired look, and a spark of pride flickered in their depths. "Thank you," she said simply.

Ambrosius steeled himself for what he had to say next. He owed them the truth.

"I am going to hunt down Vortigern," he said, "and kill him, if I can. Even with just a few followers, he is too dangerous to live, and might yet stir up more trouble for me in the west. He is also a traitor, with many British lives on his conscience. Only his death will appease all those he has betrayed."

"I wish you good hunting," replied Sevira, "and only wish I could ride with you, to see him run to earth."

Ambrosius was more concerned with her son's reaction. Pascent chewed his lower lip and said nothing. His face had paled a little.

Should I arrest him? Place him under guard? What threat can he pose?

None, was the answer. Even if he wanted to, Pascent had no means of saving his father – no soldiers, no allies, no treasure, nothing. Ambrosius suppressed the flicker of doubt in his breast, and decided to be lenient.

"Stay here, Pascent," he said, wheeling his horse, "stay here and help your mother to rebuild her home."

As he cantered away towards the villa, his father's voice echoed faintly in his head, dredged up from the musty vaults of memory.

"Soft-hearted..."

21.

Here, on the roof of the world, Vortigern was safe. He stood on the walkway of the drystone rampart and gazed at the last dying golden rays of the sun as it slowly dipped behind the mountains.

Dinas Ddraig – Fortress of the Dragon – as the fort was known, stood on a rocky, wooded hillock overlooking the southern end of Llyn Dinas, a vast lake ringed by high forests and dreaming blue mountains. The local peasants nurtured an age-old tale of dragons nesting on top of the hillock, hence its name.

The fort was originally a simple wooden palisade. Vortigern had known it as such, when he visited and played here as a child. The lord of Dinas Ddraig had been a kinsman of his, and Vortigern's father often sent him here for safe keeping, away from the tribal wars raging in the south.

Ever mindful of the need for a last redoubt in case of disaster, Vortigern had taken Dinas Ddraig for himself after his kinsman died. When he became High King, he ordered the palisade to be rebuilt in stone, with more defensive ramparts erected further down the hillside. The drystone wall was roughly circular and enclosed a number of roundhuts and outbuildings.

Now the disaster had come, and the High King, a fugitive from his own people, had fled to this lonely outpost in the heart of the remote mountains of north-west Venedotia.

He had renamed the fort. To him, if no-one else, it was now Dinas Eryr, the Fortress of the Eagle. His eagle banner flew from the battlements, a last act of defiance against the world that had rebelled against him.

"Let my enemies come," he shouted, cupping his hands round his mouth, "let them break their teeth against the mountain!" His voice echoed and re-echoed through the rocky valleys and high passes. He grinned. Up here, with the cold wind whipping across his face and making his cloak billow around him, Vortigern felt like a god.

They would come for him soon enough. He almost relished the prospect of the final battle. His sword would shatter the bone-cages of a good many warriors before they overwhelmed him, like a pack of hounds pulling down an old stag.

He drew his sword and held it upright before his eyes, gazing fondly at every nick and dint in the steel. Vortigern was old, well over sixty, but he could still fight.

The lines of an old poem, composed by a bard in honour of his youthful exploits in battle, drifted through his fractured mind.

"He glutted black ravens on the walls of the fortress,

Among the great ones in battle,

In the front rank, Vortigern was a lion, a wolf, a bear, a cruel god of war…

Not slow was his spear,

In laying low the foemen,

Full nine hundred and sixty did he slay,

He did not think it too many."

He laughed, a shrill, too-loud bark of mirth, and swung his sword through empty air. The bard was long-dead, and so were Vortigern's days of glory.

It all seemed an impossibly distant memory now: his rise to power among the Cornovii, and the rivals he had slaughtered in single combat, ripping out their entrails with his bare hands; the cattle-raids and skirmishes, night-time ambushes, hard fighting by river crossings and under the timber ramparts of hill-forts; the weight of gold on his brow as the crown was lowered onto his head for the first time; the hall-feastings that followed; the heady rush of power as men grovelled before him. All the rich fruits of earthly wealth.

"Once I was lord of all," he breathed, lowering his sword, "I could muster the greatest war-band in Britannia. Five hundred buccelari rode under my eagle banner. The earth shook under the tread of my horses. It was death to deny my will. My lightest word was law."

He rubbed his head. Perhaps his memory was at fault. He knew they had tried to restrain him, to restrict his power and make him govern through a council.

The councillors were all dead now. Their ghostly faces shimmered before his eyes. He dimly recalled them falling under Saxon knives.

"No man should question my will," he mumbled, "I am the High King, the lord of lords."

"No man should," agreed a female voice. Startled, Vortigern turned to his left, and smiled at his wife.

Rowena was no longer the shapely beauty who first entranced him, making his heart and head sing with lust until he could think of nothing else but slaking it. Her waist-length hair, once the colour of spun gold, had faded to white, but there was still a trace of her old loveliness in the plump, heart-shaped face, the bright blue eyes with long lashes, and the full red mouth.

"No man should," she repeated, stepping closer to run her fingers through his silky nest of beard, "and no man will, when you come into your power again."

Vortigern closed his eyes in ecstasy. Her touch still had the power to transport him. He had always been a slave to beautiful women, from the goat-herd's daughter who first initiated him to the mysteries of sex, to his first wife Sevira, and finally to Rowena, for the sake of whom he had forfeited the love of his people.

"You are a witch," he murmured, "I am certain of it. Your power lies in your touch, in your smile, in the light of your eyes. I broke faith with my subjects for you. With my wife and sons. I lied and schemed and murdered. All for you."

His eyes opened. "In return, what have you given me? Where have you led me?"

"I gave you my life," she answered, "my heart and soul. My body."

Vortigern scowled. "I have your brother Hengist to thank for those. He sold you to me in exchange for Cent. All those lush green acres, given up for a woman! A woman who gave me no sons. What a fool I am."

He caught her fingers in his own. They were plump and white and delicate. If he squeezed, they would easily break.

No. He could never hurt Rowena. Never escape her. Their fates were entwined. Not even death could cut the threads that bound them together.

"Courage, lord king," said Rowena, "you will come into your power again. I have seen it."

"In the stones," he sneered, turning away to resume his vigil of the mountains. The heavy gold light of the dying sun had darkened to crimson, bathing Dinas Eryr in a blood-red afterglow.

"Yes," she replied, "the runestones. They never lie."

Vortigern was half-convinced, half-repelled by his wife's belief in the power of the runes, a series of unintelligible marks scratched onto a handful of pebbles she kept in a velvet bag hanging from her waist. When she cast the stones on the ground, Rowena claimed to be able to read the future from the patterns they formed.

"I cast the runes this morning," she said, "they spoke of your final victory. A victory forged in fire, on the hill of the dragon."

He gazed down the craggy sides of the hillock. "No dragons dwell here now," he replied quietly, "only eagles."

The next morning found him back at his post, watching the mountains to the east. Soon, he expected to glimpse the flash of sunlight on advancing spears.

Vortigern, who once commanded a thousand men in battle, now had twenty-six to help him defend the fort. Of these, twelve had followed him from Londinium, while the rest made up Dinas Eryr's permanent garrison. The latter had remained loyal to the High King and held onto their lofty stronghold, even though the rest of Venedotia was in the hands of Cunedda, King of the Votadini.

Thus far, Cunedda had not tried to take the fort. The place was practically unassailable, and the Votadini could ill-afford to commit their warriors to a lengthy siege. Cunedda needed all his spears to defend Venedotia's coastline against the ravages of the Scotti.

AMBROSIUS

Vortigern was not fool enough to imagine he would be left in peace. Sooner or later Ambrosius would come and join his forces to those of Cunedda, his friend and ally.

Ambrosius. The name was like a curse, a portent of dread. Vortigern had not seen the man since Guoloph, and even then only from afar.

For decades, Ambrosius had been a lurking menace in the west, constantly disrupting Vortigern's plans and providing a safe haven for his enemies. He had proved impossible to kill. None of the assassins Vortigern sent to put an end to his enemy had returned, save one, whose headless body Ambrosius sent back to Londinium tied to the back of an ass.

Vortigern was resigned to his fate. His doom had been long in coming, but he had always known it was unavoidable. The Treachery of the Long Knives, his greatest folly, had condemned him in the eyes of God and man. Now he merely waited for the end.

Shortly after noon, the sentry on the tower glimpsed the long-awaited spears. Vortigern joined him on the rampart.

He shaded his eyes against the sun, beating down mercilessly from a pure blue sky. A mile or so to the east, he saw banners and spear-heads advancing through a narrow defile. A cloud of dust hovered over them, stirred up by the passage of hundreds of men and horses.

The land immediately to the south-east of Dinas Eryr was flat, and divided by a shallow river. Part of the forest was cleared away for pasture. Vortigern watched in silence as the enemy host slowly emerged from the woods beyond the defile and spread out to deploy on the open ground beside the river.

His sight was dimmed with age, but it wasn't difficult to pick out Ambrosius. The Dux Bellorum cut an almost regal figure, clad in a flowing purple cloak and mounted on a white horse at the head of his silver-mailed buccelari, the dragon standard billowing above his head.

Vortigern could have wept. At the height of his strength and power, he had appeared no less splendid, though he never presumed to wear the purple. Ambrosius inherited that right from his Roman forebears, themselves jumped-up civil servants with pretensions to senatorial rank.

"Will you call yourself Caesar when I am dead, Ambrosius?" said Vortigern, "will you take your armies over the sea, to try and revive the diseased corpse of the Western Empire?"

Vortigern dearly hoped so. He wanted Ambrosius to meet the same fate as the other failed pretenders before him, Maximus and Constantine. Let him succumb to vainglorious dreams of empire, and take his troops over the sea, to meet death at the hands of treacherous Romans or savage Visigoths.

Lord, let Ambrosius perish on some foreign battlefield, he prayed, *and leave Britannia to a native prince. Let the last traces of Roman power die with him.*

Vortigern ordered his sentry to sound the war-horn, summoning the garrison to arms. His warriors came scrambling from the barracks and quickly filled the walkway of the fort's southern rampart.

Rowena came too, dressed like a Saxon shield-maiden from some epic saga, wearing a shirt sewn with shimmering iron scales over her gown. She had pulled her long hair back into a single plait, and carried a heavy ash spear in both hands.

Vortigern's heart lifted at the sight of her. "Did you think I would skulk indoors?" she said, taking her place by his side, "waiting for our enemies to batter down the gates? We shall fight and die together."

Vortigern took her hand. They believed in different gods – he had never succeeded in coaxing Rowena away from her pagan idols – but felt certain their souls would find each other in the afterlife.

"If my love for you offends Christ," he whispered, "then so be it. I could endure all the torments of Hell, so long as you were beside me."

The clamour of bugles and drums from below recalled him to his duty. He looked down and watched the enemy move into position. Ambrosius had brought some five to six hundred spearmen, red-cloaked infantry mixed with tattooed Votadini warriors, and two hundred cavalry.

AMBROSIUS

Vortigern cursed when he saw the artillery being unloaded from a train of ox-drawn wagons to the rear. Ballistas, catapults, even an onager or two, almost certainly taken from the walls of Viroconium.

The garrison of Vortigern's tribal capital had refused him entry, saying they feared the wrath of Ambrosius. They had betrayed their lord, and given his enemy the means to break down the walls of his last stronghold.

Vortigern drew his sword. "Take courage, soldiers!" he shouted, "pay no heed to the noise made by those pigs below. When the time for fighting comes, we shall meet them blade to blade!"

His men failed to muster a cheer in response. They looked sullen and furtive, their eyes full of fear as they gazed down at the overwhelming numbers of the enemy host.

"What's the matter with you?" he raged, "you are warriors, oath-sworn to the High King, not a pack of timorous old women! Raise your voices to Heaven, and let those whoresons know they are in for a fight!"

He saw two of his spearmen exchange glances. Then, as if in unspoken agreement, they calmly laid down their spears and shields and ran down the flight of timber steps beside the gate.

"Traitors!" Vortigern howled, "cravens, deserters! Return to your posts, or I'll have your heads!"

He howled in vain. More men followed, laying aside their weapons and joining the original deserters in lifting the heavy bar of the gate. That done, they stampeded through the gateway, following the steep path on the western side of the hillock leading down to the lower ramparts and the river.

Vortigern was left with just his wife for company. Stunned by this final betrayal, he could only watch as the mob of deserters splashed across the river, holding up their hands in surrender.

His last hope that was Ambrosius would slaughter the lot of them. Cowards and turncoats deserved no less.

Ambrosius lacked the High King's taste for blood. Instead of killing the deserters, he had some of his spearmen take them prisoner, binding their wrists and leading them away to the rear.

"God curse them," hissed Vortigern, "God curse them all. Where is my final victory now?"

"Patience, my love," she murmured, "I have seen it in the runes. I have seen you crowned in fire. They do not lie."

Vortigern expected Ambrosius to send a troop of cavalry up the path to search for him. He would not hide, or allow himself to be taken prisoner and paraded in triumph through the streets of Londinium.

The shadow of death was near. Vortigern thought he could see it, slanting across Rowena's face. She smiled bravely at him, and they kissed for the last time on earth.

Ambrosius came in person, cantering up the steep slope at the head of ten buccelari. They halted before the lower gates, where he dismounted and walked on alone.

Vortigern snatched Rowena's spear. "I am here, Roman!" he cried, drawing back the spear to throw, "have you come to gloat over me? Step closer, and I will put a length of sharp iron through your body!"

Ambrosius stopped, looked up at Vortigern, and slowly raised his hands to unfasten the ties of his crested helmet, which had a nose-guard and dangling cheek-pieces.

He lifted off the helmet, and for the first time Vortigern beheld the face of his enemy. It was much as he imagined. Clean-shaven, lean and hard, with cold, piercing eyes and a thin stubble of grey hair, shaved in Roman military style.

The cold eyes lingered on Vortigern for a few seconds, and then on Rowena.

"Vortigern," said Ambrosius in the sharp, clipped tones of one born to command, "I will not bandy words. Surrender, and I will give you a far cleaner death than you deserve. The life of Rowena shall be spared."

"And if I do not?" Vortigern replied scornfully, lowering his spear. It was clear Ambrosius had no intention of venturing within range.

"If not, you burn. Fire shall consume this fortress, with you and your mate locked inside it."

"None shall mourn you," he added in a softer voice, "save your last son, Pascent. He is alive, and dwelling in peace with his mother."

Mention of Pascent re-ignited the simmering rage in Vortigern's breast. "Am I expected to be grateful for that?" he roared, "you, who turned my other sons against me and led them to their deaths. Do you expect a word of thanks?"

Ambrosius tucked his helmet under the crook of his arm. "I did nothing," he replied sadly, "the fault is all yours, Vortigern. Vortimer and Catigern chose to die defending the people their father had betrayed. As you sowed, so you must reap."

"Rot to Hell, you sanctimonious prig!" Vortimer yelled, and hurled his spear in a last, desperate effort to strike down the man he loathed and feared above all others.

Age had robbed his arm of much of its strength, and the spear stuck into the ground well short of its target. Ambrosius glanced at it in weary contempt.

"I appeal to you," he said, "see sense. Let your wife go. Upon my oath, she will come to no harm." "Your oath is not worth dung," sneered Vortigern, "not even if you swore on your father's soul. I remember his death, Ambrosius. He drowned in his own blood, choking for air as he tried to plead for mercy. Begging me, on his knees, even as his blood drained onto the grass!"

The pathetic barb failed to sting. Ambrosius' stern features betrayed no trace of anger. "Once more, and for the last time, I ask you to release Rowena. I will not have it said that I murdered a woman."

"I am not my husband's prisoner," cried Rowena, "I choose to stay with him. It would take a far better man than you to drag us apart."

Even this failed to make a dent in Ambrosius' infuriating self-assurance. Without another word he donned his helmet, turned smartly on his heel and marched away. The gate swung shut behind him.

"Come, my lady," said Vortigern, taking his wife's hand. Side by side, as though walking to a feast held in their honour, they walked primly down the steps to the inner ward.

The thunder of drums sounded behind them as they approached the largest of the cluster of roundhuts, where Vortigern had his lodgings.

It was rough comfort inside, more suited to a slave than a king, with a bare earth floor and no frescoes or wall hangings to hide the dirty interior of the wattle-and-daub walls. Smoke from the fire, currently unlit, escaped through a hole cut into the thatched roof.

"I like this place," Rowena had said when she first saw her new home, "I was born in a hut very much like it. The circle of my life is complete."

There was little furniture, save a straw-stuffed mattress on the floor covered in plaids, and a small bench in the middle of the room. Two three-legged stools were arranged either side of the bench.

Vortigern politely handed his wife to her seat before taking his opposite. A pair of wooden cups and an earthenware jug half-full of cloudy mead stood on the bench between them. He reached for the jug.

Something landed with a thump outside, making the fragile walls of the hut shudder. Ambrosius' artillery had started to bombard the fort.

Unconcerned, Vortigern poured out two measures of mead and gave Rowena one of the cups.

"Your health," he said, raising his own cup in salute, before tossing the contents down his throat. Rowena sipped more delicately.

They drank the jug dry while flaming missiles and fire-arrows rained down on Dinas Eryr. The thatch on the roundhouses was first to catch light, and the crackling flames quickly spread, rippling over the dry mud of the walls and leaping from roof to roof, mingled with suffocating clouds of grey smoke.

God spared Vortigern's hut until last. None of the sacks of burning coals flung by the onagers hit the roof, but one or two of the fire-arrows lodged in the thatch. That was enough to start a flame, while questing tendrils of smoke crept through the open doorway.

Vortigern and Rowena sat and waited for death.

Gobbets of burning thatch dropped onto the floor, and the room slowly filled up with smoke and whirling sparks.

The sparks are like stars, Vortigern thought dreamily. Smoke was getting into his nostrils and making his eyes water. His vision of Rowena blurred, but he could still feel her hands, joined with his across the bench.

*A victory forged in fire...*so Rowena had promised. She had seen it in the stones, and they never lied. Here was no victory, unless depriving Ambrosius of his body counted as such. Vortigern's flesh, and his wife's, would melt and slough from their bones, releasing their souls to spend eternity together, fused as one among the stars.

Entranced by this vision, Vortigern barely heard the creaking of the rafters above his head, or felt the chunk of smouldering wood that broke away and landed on the back of his skull.

He toppled onto his face, scattering the jug and the cups, and only dimly heard the anguished screams of his wife. Her voice steadily diminished, as did the sensation of pain in his smoke-filled lungs and the strange numbness in his head.

Everything fell away, vanishing down a dark tunnel, while he was pulled towards a tiny glimmer of white light. A candle hanging in the sky. Vortigern tried to grasp it, but the light was snuffed out by some unseen hand.

He plunged into darkness.

22.

The wars had ceased. Like a man emerging from the horrors of a long, life-threatening sickness, Britannia slowly recovered.

Vortigern was dead, Hengist fled, and the Saxons penned up in their stolen lands in the eastern half of the island. Ambrosius saw it as his task to mend the ruin, and make Britannia once again a wealthy, secure, well-governed Roman province.

He was all too aware of the limited time left to him. Ambrosius was forty-six, a good age in a time when most men were fortunate to each fifty, and knew he had reached the winter of his days.

"If God allows, maybe I can live another ten years," he said, "even five would be sufficient. By then, I think, you will be ready."

He looked sharply at Artorius. The young man was now eighteen, only a little older than Ambrosius when he rode out on his first command.

"You will live many years yet, father," Artorius replied, yawning and stretching his long arms until the shoulder-bones clicked, "you are like the pillars of the earth. Nothing knocks you down."

You could, thought Ambrosius, *and with ease.*

It was difficult to align the giant youth sitting opposite him with the scruffy, underfed waif he had first rescued from a beating at Curia, all those years ago. Artorius was already over six feet tall, and had plenty of growing left to do. His lean body was all muscle and sinew, the result of ceaseless exercise and a frugal military diet. Unlike many warriors, he seldom drank to excess. There was a quiet, self-contained discipline about him, which Ambrosius liked to think stemmed from his teaching.

If he carries on sprouting, he will grow to be as big as Horsa, and an even better warrior. He is British and Roman, with the finest martial qualities of both peoples blended into one.

I made him. I forged him. Artorius is my legacy to Britannia.

AMBROSIUS

The young man's mop of tawny gold hair shone in the candlelight. He wore it long to his shoulders, and was attempting to grow a beard, which would serve to hide his somewhat heavy jaw-line. Artorius' face was strong rather than handsome, with prominent cheekbones and a fleshy, aquiline nose. His steely grey eyes brooded inside deep sockets. Their stern aspect was softened slightly by the fringe of fair hair falling over his wide brow.

They were sitting at the round table, inside the vast, shadowy rotunda in the old Roman governor's palace in Londinium, where the Council of Britannia used to meet. Ambrosius fancied he could sense their ghosts, whispering at his shoulder.

He occupied his father's old seat, while Artorius had chosen a seat at random. The rest were vacant. Ambrosius refused to even look at the high-backed chair of dark polished wood once occupied by the High King. Vortigern's shade seemed to fill the room, influencing everything that was said.

"I will form a new council," said Ambrosius, "the province cannot be governed or administered properly without one. New men shall be chosen to fill these seats. You, Artorius, shall be the first of my appointments. Eidol Cadarn and Cunedda shall also sit at the round table. Cunedda's son, Cadwallon Lawhir, shall be another. Men I can trust."

"I'm honoured," replied Artorius with a lazy smile, "do I get a title, and some nice fat lands to go with it?"

"A title, certainly, but a military one to suit your role as my successor. Magister Equitum. You are the best horseman among my buccelari, so you may as well lead them. No lands. Yours will be a roving commission, and I don't want you tied down to one part of the country."

"Or," he added with a smile of his own, "entertaining dreams of power. We have more than enough petty kings and chieftains to cope with."

Artorius accepted the mild rebuke with good grace. His true thoughts were hard to discern. Dangerous when roused, he could also be subtle, and was fast learning how to manipulate his fellow man.

"What of the High Kingship?" he asked, studying his nails, "that old chair can't stay empty forever."

"I'm tempted to have it chopped up and burned as firewood," Ambrosius replied sourly, "there will be no more High Kings. Vortigern tried to treat the councillors as advisors, ultimately subject to his authority. When he realised they wouldn't let him rule as he wished, he conspired with Hengist to have them murdered. No good comes of placing one man above all others, and investing him with divine authority."

"Someone must rule, though," said Artorius, "it all comes down to one man in the end."

"You are the Dux Bellorum," he added, giving Ambrosius a meaningful look, "the only man left in Britannia with the power and authority to rule. It has to be you."

"No," Ambrosius said stubbornly, "my power rests entirely on the army. I won't be some latter-day barracks emperor, ruling unchecked until the soldiers tire of me, and set up someone else in my stead."

He didn't need to add who his obvious replacement would be. Artorius was maturing fast, slightly too fast for Ambrosius' liking. Already a fine soldier and superb horseman, with the respect and liking of the troops under his command, he might soon start to chafe in his subordinate role.

There was a strong bond of mutual trust and affection between Ambrosius and his adopted son, but he held no illusions. Artorius had risen high in a short time. It was only natural he should feel the tug of ambition. At just eighteen years of age, he found himself second only to the Dux Bellorum. No other man dared meet his eye. How far might he rise yet?

The answer, Ambrosius reckoned, was to keep him busy. "As Magister Equitum, you will be responsible for the cavalry arm of the comitatenses," he said, "you will be based here in the capital, ready to ride out at a moment's notice." Artorius nodded. He fully understood his role, and how Ambrosius planned to turn Britannia into a fortified camp, an extension of the complex system of defences he and his father had set up in the west. The Saxon and Pictish frontiers would be guarded by a chain of newly-built forts, with beacons and towers set up on the hills to watch for raiders from the sea and war-bands seeking to drive further into British territory.

Ambrosius had based his plan on the Roman model. The limitanei garrisoning the forts were responsible for dealing with small-scale raids, and for lighting the beacons to give advance warning of more serious incursions. The local chieftains or magistrates would lead their household warriors and citizen levies to aid the limitanei in repelling the threat. If their combined forces proved inadequate, gallopers would be sent to summon Artorius and his elite cavalry.

This triple layer of defences should be enough, Ambrosius hoped, to contain Britannia's enemies inside their own borders. In time, when the Britons had recovered their former strength and prosperity, they would be able to push the Saxons out of the east and reclaim their lost lands.

The Wall would continue to be partially defended, but the Britons lacked the men to garrison all the abandoned forts along its eighty-mile length. Coel Hen was dead, and another governor was needed to replace him at Eburucum. Ambrosius was toying with the idea of going north himself for a while, to oversee the construction of his new defences. Perhaps another of the northern tribes could be summoned from beyond the Wall, to re-settle in the more fertile land to the south and provide men for the limitanei.

Strictly speaking, his presence in the north was unnecessary. He could easily send a subordinate – a northerner, perhaps, such as Cei or Bedwyr, who knew the land and its people – and Ambrosius could do far more good if he stayed in Londinium, the centre of government.

In truth, he wanted to see the north country again, and feel the cold lash of wind and rain on his face. To Ambrosius, the north was another world, and offered an escape from his cares and troubles.

He had lost Helena. Weary of being a soldier's wife, she had left Mons Ambrius for good, to join their daughter in the convent on the remote western coast of Dumnonia.

"I must be with Morgana," she had told him before departing, "and God. You have no further use for me."

Ambrosius reacted angrily, the more so since it helped to mask an unforgivable sense of relief. "You are my wife," he said, "we have been together since we were young. Would you abandon me now, in my declining years?"

It was no use. Helena knew him too well. "I am not abandoning you," she replied calmly, "you are welcome to visit us whenever you can spare the time."

Whenever you can spare the time. The words cut him like a knife. Ambrosius knew he had rarely made the time for his family, always putting what he regarded as his duty first.

"Besides," she added as he fought for words, "you shall not be alone. You have Artorius. He is the son I never managed to give you."

"Helena…" he began, but there was nothing more to be said. Why deny the truth? His wife and daughter were burdens on his conscience, troublesome distractions from the real work of his life. Artorius was a central part of that.

"Good-bye, Ambrosius," said Helena, gently stroking his cheek. For the rest of his days he often felt the ghost of her touch, and missed her presence in his cold bed at night.

Ambrosius put his hand to his cheek now, in the shadowy coolness of the rotunda. Marching footsteps rang in the corridor outside. The guard was changing.

He had tried to fill the abandoned palace with his own followers, but it was still a vast, echoing, half-deserted mausoleum. The same description could be applied to Londinium in general. There simply weren't enough people to occupy the city. Most of them huddled in the western quarter, leaving the rest to fall into decay.

Ambrosius was determined not to let the capital go the same way as so many other British towns and cities, and fall into disrepair. Londinium had once been a great port, and was the key to re-establishing trade with the rest of the Western Empire. Britannia did not lack for goods to export. The land yielded rich reserves of coal and tin, copper and iron ore, timber, wheat and seed oil. Only the will and the courage was needed to make the best use of them.

One of Ambrosius' first tasks was to coax people back from the countryside, to fill the empty streets and public buildings with life again, and set workmen to repairing the crumbling walls. Find crews to build new merchant vessels and mend the old, and sail them to the ports of Gaul and Amorica.

Flavius Aetius, the great Roman general and conqueror of Attila, was dead, murdered by his own Emperor, but had managed to restore a semblance of order in Gaul before he was betrayed. Thanks to him, there was hope for Roman civilisation across the Narrow Sea.

All Ambrosius needed was time, a few more years, to make Britannia rich and secure. He prayed for God to grant him that time, and preserve him from the fickle whims of fate.

"What of Hengist?" asked Artorius, breaking in on the older man's thoughts, "have there been any recent sightings of him? Last I heard, he was still alive, and lurking off the coast near Anderidum."

Ambrosius sighed. Hengist was another ghost, a shadow haunting both his dreams and waking hours.

Shortly after the death of Vortigern, the Saxon chief had quit his last refuge on the Isle of Tanatos, and sailed off into the mists of rumour and legend. There had been a few glimpses of him since, few of them confirmed. Ambrosius' scouts reported seeing him at the head of the occasional band of pirates. Never more than a few men, raiding isolated farms and fishing villages before retreating back to their ships.

Hengist might no longer pose a serious threat to Britannia's security, but he had done enough to earn a place in her nightmares. Feared and reviled by the natives, especially the ignorant common folk, he had become something of a living folk-tale, a demonic bogeyman figure, used by tired British mothers to frighten their children to sleep.

"I have heard nothing of Hengist recently," he replied, "he could well be dead. Let us pray so. The recent sighting may have been one of his sons. They should be of an age to lead their own war-bands by now."

He clenched his fist. "There is no end to these damned barbarians. They breed like vermin."

Artorius looked amused. "Indeed. As a barbarian myself, I should know. Though my father only had one son."

"Both your fathers," Ambrosius reminded him, "you are mine, every bit as much as Uthyr's. I wish you would forget him. Dwelling on your forefathers encourages sentiment, and might lead you to favour the Selgovae over other British tribes. You cannot afford to have favourites. When I die, you will succeed me, and must be just and even-handed to all."

Artorius spread his hands. "So you admit it. You will rule alone. But as what, father? If you won't govern as Dux Bellorum, and refuse the High Kingship, what title will you take?"

Ambrosius had no answer. An awkward silence fell, and Vortigern's empty chair seemed to grow in stature until its shadow filled the room.

23.

Morgana dreamed. In her dream she saw a star streaking through the heavens. The star was on fire, and trailed a long beam of light behind it, like the tail of a dragon.

The star hovered over Britannia, bathing the island in fiery red light. Gradually the light faded, and the star grew cold, a mere chunk of rock spinning aimlessly in the night sky.

Deprived of its protection, Britannia also grew cold and lifeless. The shadows threatening it from all directions rolled across the land, swallowing up the good earth and the people that dwelled on it, leaving nothing but desolation. Britannia became a dead land, a mass cemetery, with no flicker of life remaining on its blasted surface.

She woke with a start. Her hands groped blindly in the dark, and felt the reassuring touch of the rough stone of her cell. The abbess had insisted on taking Morgana out of the dormitory and giving her a private bedchamber. She had woken the other nuns with her screams too often, and had to be removed before she became a disruptive influence.

It was the pit of night, with no moon. All was darkness beyond the narrow slit window opposite her bed. She might have fastened the wooden shutters, but if she did that Morgana felt trapped, a prisoner inside a tiny stone dungeon.

She was a prisoner anyway, condemned to remain inside this convent until she died. The abbess had always been kind to her, but firm, and never let her venture beyond the walls.

"The world is cold, and full of danger," she would say, patting Morgana's hand, "you are too delicate to survive out there. Morgana, our most precious jewel. I could never forgive myself if some harm came to you."

She sat on the edge of her narrow bed and tried to interpret her dream. It was another of her prophecies, of that Morgana was certain. She was experiencing them more often these days, at prayer and while asleep.

The cell was cold. She was only wearing a thin woollen shift, and her skin prickled into goosebumps. Morgana ignored the discomfort and pressed her knuckles to her sightless eyes, trying to think.

Slowly, the answers came to her. *The star is my father. He covers the land in his light, pressing back the darkness, shielding Britannia from her enemies.*

The star grows old. His death shall be sudden, and Britannia left defenceless. The darkness shall engulf us.

But...

Her thoughts turned to Artorius, whose fame had penetrated even the thick walls of the convent. All knew he was the ageing Ambrosius' right arm, his sword and shield in the never-ending war against the barbarians. The land would not be left without a defender once Ambrosius died. His able successor would step into the breach.

Morgana chewed her lip. Artorius was the red dragon of prophecy, who would cast his white rival into the sea. She had believed this for years, and taken comfort from it.

Prophecies can change.

This new voice was the merest breath of a whisper inside her head. It was not her own. She had heard it before, but only as mere fragments of words and phrases. Now it spoke clearly to her.

The Kings of Britannia will not accept Artorius. To them he is a mere soldier, a jumped-up nobody with the blood of northern savages in his veins. Even now they conspire against him.

Suddenly Morgana understood what she had to do. The knowledge trickled into her brain like a flow of ice-cold water, awakening her to her true purpose.

She got up and dressed in the dark, with none of the awkward fumbling that usually accompanied even her most basic functions.

The door slid open at her touch, and she ghosted down the stone-flagged passage outside. Morgana felt herself guided, as though led by some invisible hand.

She paused by the entrance to the dormitory. The door was closed, and beyond lay the sisters she had lived alongside for over two-thirds of her life.

Among them was her mother. Helena had come to the convent to spend her last years in the company of her daughter. Morgana hesitated, not wanting to leave without even a parting word.

No. There can be no delay. Come.

Morgana flitted down the corridor. She was a shadow among shadows, barely alive, having shed the skin of her old life. The spirit that commanded her, spoke to her, would ensure she passed from the convent undetected.

It was the moving spirit of the land, and Morgana was now its servant.

24.

Another four years passed, years of relative peace and plenty. Under the careful guidance of Ambrosius, Britannia grew rich and strong again. The Council of Britannia was re-established, but he could never quite escape the need for a strong unifying figure to lead the councillors and rule the land through them.

Ambrosius was exhausted. He wanted to retire, to lay aside the burden of duty and spend his last days with his family. Or, like many prominent soldiers before him, enter a monastery and make his final peace with God.

Peace was denied him. There was always some additional task or crisis to deal with: ruffled tempers on the council, a blood-feud between squabbling tribes, savage raids over the Wall, Saxon incursions from the debated lands in the east.

Artorius, the Magister Equitum, was indispensable. He and his buccelari rode up and down the country, responding to every midnight beacon and panicky rumour of sea-raiders.

Tales filtered back to Londinium of their exploits. Artorius' men were like wolves, hunting down invading barbarian war-bands with merciless ferocity, ambushing them in the grey light of dawn as they slept, killing all they found. Occasionally he allowed a few survivors to flee back to their ships, so they might sail away and spread word of what awaited those who sought to ravage Britannia.

Ambrosius was cheered by his adopted son's military success, but less with his behaviour in council. Artorius was loudest among those who pressured him, demanding that he take the title of High King. Others included Cunedda and Eidol Cadarn, whom Ambrosius had always considered friends.

"It is for your sake that we urge you to take the crown," said Cunedda, whose shock of red hair was now streaked with white, "you cannot rule safely otherwise."

"That is what the priests are calling you," put in Cadwallon, his son, "without the sanctity of a crown, many consider you a mere soldier, with no true claim to authority."

AMBROSIUS

This was what Ambrosius wished to avoid: to be regarded as a *superbus tyrannus*, a tyrant without legitimate power, entirely dependent on control of the army.

He acknowledged the force of these arguments, but would not agree to wear a crown. He regarded the High Kingship as an outdated absurdity, dredged up from the mire of Britannia's past before the legions came. As a true-born Roman, who dreamed of seeing the Western Empire restored to its full glory, he could never assume an office that dragged Britannia further away from the light of Roman civilisation.

Matters came to a head when he entered the rotunda one morning to find the entire council assembled to greet him.

Silence reigned in the chamber. Every man stood by his place at the table, save Cunedda and Artorius, who knelt facing the doorway. Between them they held a purple cushion, and on the cushion rested a slender band of dark red gold. It was forged in the shape of a laurel wreath, of the kind once worn by Roman Emperors.

Ambrosius eyed the wreath with loathing. It was the crown of the High King, and had once adorned Vortigern's brow. Ever since the latter's death it had lain gathering dust in a strong-room under the palace.

"What is this trinket you have brought before me?" Ambrosius cried, "take it away!"

"Lord," said Artorius, unmoved, "we beseech you to take the crown. The land cries out for a strong ruler, a just man with the power to unite the tribes and heal old wounds."

In a rare flash of temper, Ambrosius plucked the wreath from the cushion and hurled it against the wall. It bounced off the stone with a hollow clang and rolled away across the floor, eventually coming to rest against a chair leg.

"Melt the worthless thing down," he shouted, his voice echoing in the high dome of the ceiling, "and have it turned into plate, so I may eat my dinner off it. Otherwise I never wish to clap eyes on it again."

He had cause to regret his outburst. Most of the new councillors were younger men, and regarded themselves as

209

Britons rather than Romans. For them, the title of High King had a mystical, almost sacred quality, and the wreath was a precious symbol of the highest office in the land. None dared to openly challenge Ambrosius or raise a voice in protest, but he saw the ugly looks on their faces, and knew he had made a terrible blunder.

Eventually, realising the difficulty of his position, he thought to resurrect the title of Vicarius. This was at least a Roman office, bestowed on the governor of Britannia in the latter days of the Roman occupation, who in turn reported to the Prefect in Gaul. A purely administrative role, with no false glamour of High Kingship, it enabled Ambrosius to preside over the council with supreme civilian as well as military status.

His decision pleased no-one. "The office of Vicarius no longer has any meaning," Cunedda complained in private, "there is no Prefect in Gaul anymore. Even if there was, why should you report to him? Rome abandoned us decades ago. The Empire no longer has any say in our affairs."

"You know very well I mean to re-establish Britannia as a Roman province," Ambrosius said patiently, "when the time is right, I shall send envoys to Anthemius, and offer to aid him in driving the Visigoths from Gaul. Together our combined forces shall sweep the West clean of barbarians."

Cunedda looked doubtful. Anthemius was the latest in the long and not very successful line of Western Emperors, following the poisoning of his predecessor, Libius Severus. An able soldier, he was making some progress against the Visigoths who had descended like a plague on Gaul, taking advantage of Roman weakness to overrun large chunks of territory. They were kin to the Saxons, and possessed much the same freebooting instincts.

"You place too much faith in Anthemius," said Cunedda, "he won't last long. None of the Caesars do. Like his predecessors, he cares nothing for Britannia. What are we to him? A damp little ex-province in the far north of the civilised world, infested with barbarians."

Ambrosius would not listen. He was growing old, and his body was weakening. For the past three winters he had suffered from a debilitating cough, and spent much of the darkest time of year confined to his bed, scarcely able to breathe. His condition improved with the onset of spring, but every year his recovery was slower and more difficult. Death was on the horizon, but appeared to be in no hurry.

Just a little while longer, lord, Ambrosius prayed, *until Artorius has come fully of age. Until there is peace in the land. Until the council learns to govern without me. Until...*

There was no end to his labours, no time in which he felt it safe to relinquish his grip. Worrying reports started to reach the council of a rise in the number of Saxon raids. There were even attacks on the British forts Ambrosius had built to guard the eastern frontier. The attacks ended in failure, but the renewed boldness of the Saxons was disturbing.

"A new generation of warriors has grown up," said Ambrosius, "who wish to avenge the defeats suffered by their fathers.

He crossed himself. "God save us from the fury of the sons of Hengist."

Too unwell to ride to war himself, Ambrosius now relied entirely on his adopted son to hold the line against the barbarians. At the end of the campaigning season Artorius returned to Londinium, battered and war-weary, with news of the Saxon chiefs he had spent months fighting.

"Their main leaders are Osla, whom they call Big-Knife, and Ebusa," he told the council, "Hengist's sons by two different mothers. He has many wives."

His heavy features darkened. "There is a third, not so powerful as the others, but more intelligent. Cerdic. Their half-brother, and reputedly the son of a British slave-woman raped by Hengist. Cerdic is a shrewd one. He sticks to the marshes and waterways and lays clever ambushes for our cavalry. I lost many good men thanks to him."

"I saw nothing of Hengist himself," he added, "though the Saxon prisoners we took seem to think he is not dead. They speak of him and his brother Horsa as gods, who will one day cross the sea to reclaim their lost land."

"The land in question being Cent," said Ambrosius, "which Hengist tricked Vortigern into giving him in exchange for his whore of a sister."

He rubbed his tired eyes. Some of the younger men of the council were watching him with a mixture of indifference and barely-concealed boredom.

How much of a relic I must look and sound to them, he thought wryly, *the people I speak of are part of history. Mere dust. Hengist, Vortigern, Rowena...they are all gone now, slipped into shadow. Only I remain, clinging to life and power like a limpet.*

A relic. The last of the Romans. Ambrosius looked at the youthful faces around him and realised his time was gone. The rotting hulk of the Western Empire could not be saved, and Britannia would never be restored as a Roman province.

Rome had become unfashionable. The younger members of the council preferred to hark back to native customs and dress, and regarded themselves as Britons first. They looked and sounded barbaric to Ambrosius, decked in their garish finery, torcs and rings and arm-bands, keen on boasting of their exploits in bed and battle.

Many were skilled storytellers – or liars – and claimed to possess the most bizarre and illogical attributes. Henwas Edeiniog, for instance, liked to claim that no four-legged animal could ever keep pace with him over one acre, let alone beyond that. Another, Henbeddestyr, reckoned he could outrun any man, whether on horseback or on foot. Then there was Gilla Goeshydd, who had Scotti blood in his veins, and claimed to be the chief leaper of Hibernia, able to clear three hundred acres in a single bound. No-one ever asked to put these ludicrous boasts to the test: it was considered discourteous.

Ambrosius moved on to study the men sitting beside Artorius. Cei, Bedwyr and Gwalchmei. These three had grown closest to his adopted son, their differences forgotten in the heat of battle. Strangers to humility, they liked to call themselves the Three Chief Warriors of the Island of the Mighty.

Cei concerned him most. The redhead was loyal, but suffered from touchy pride and an ungovernable temper. Ambrosius recalled what Cei's father, a crippled old Votadini warrior named Cynr Ceinfarfog, had once told him of his son.

"If there is any part of me in my son, lord, his heart will always be cold, and there will be no warmth in his soul. He will be stubborn. No-one will withstand war and hardship as well as Cei. Nor will there be any servant or officer as good as him."

Cold-hearted, quick-tempered, stubborn and loyal. Artorius would do well to watch Cei, and do all he could to keep him happy.

Ambrosius made a decision. It rose out of nowhere, from gut instinct rather than his head. He would rule for another year, a twelvemonth, and then retire at the end of the following summer. All his power, and the title of Vicarius, would be passed on to Artorius.

His adopted son was twenty-two now, a tough, seasoned warlord and father to an infant son by his favourite concubine, Ganhumara. He was ready to fulfil his destiny.

Ambrosius kept his decision a secret, intending to complete one final task before announcing his withdrawal from public life. When he was gone, Artorius would need the full and unequivocal support of all the great ones of Britannia. There could be no bad blood, no lingering grudges.

To that end, Ambrosius made strenuous efforts to reconcile Vortigern's surviving family and supporters with his regime. He sent gifts of weapons and horses to the Cornovii, who had never acknowledged his authority, and a message to Pascent, inviting him and his widowed mother to court.

Ambrosius had kept a careful watch on Pascent over the years, but the last of Vortigern's sons never gave him any cause for doubt or fear. He seemed content to live quietly in the country with Sevira, helping her to rebuild the shattered family estates.

A seat on the council had fallen vacant. The previous occupant had died in battle against a Scotti war-band, and Ambrosius had decided to take the risk of offering it to Pascent.

Ambrosius' cough returned with the onset of the cold weather. This fresh reminder of his mortality spurred him into action. He ordered the council to meet on the First of November, his birthday. The date seemed appropriate, since it would mark one of his last significant acts before retirement.

He endured the humiliation of leaning on a slave's shoulder as he made the short trip from his private chambers to the rotunda. His cough, accompanied by a mild fever, had left him desperately weak and unable to walk unaided.

"Leave me be," he gasped, pushing away the slave when they reached the arched doorway to the rotunda, "I must stand before the council."

Ambrosius leaned against the wall and gathered his strength. A thin trickle of blood dribbled down the side of his mouth. He dabbed it away with a corner of his cloak.

He stretched out his right hand. Understanding, one of the sentries guarding the door handed him a spear.

Using the spear as a crutch, he hobbled into the rotunda, where he was almost knocked backwards by a wave of noise. The entire council was assembled, all but one of the twenty-five seats filled, and the councillors were on their feet, cheering and applauding the man who had held Britannia safe in the bowl of his hands for so long.

Ambrosius stood under the arch, swaying slightly, looking at each man in turn. His old friends gazed back at him warmly, and this time there was no sign of contempt on the faces of the younger men. Perhaps sensing his time was limited, they had all gathered to do him honour.

His adopted son stepped forward – strong, martial Artorius, glowing with youth and fierce vitality – and gripped his forearm. Artorius' fingers were like velvet over steel, and could have snapped the old man's brittle bones with ease.

"Come, father," said Artorius, smiling, "take your seat."

Much against his better judgment, Ambrosius had been persuaded to assume Vortigern's old chair. He limped towards it with trepidation, and thought he glimpsed the shade of his old enemy, horribly burned and blackened, sitting in his place and grinning at him.

Ambrosius suffered another fit of coughing as he lowered himself into the chair. The slave who had followed him into the rotunda handed him a white cloth. He pressed it to his mouth, wracked with painful convulsions and unable to speak, until the fit had passed.

While he coughed, the applause died down and the councillors resumed their seats. Ambrosius felt twenty-four pairs of eyes watching him with...what? Fear, anxiety, hope?

"Well, my friends," he said breathlessly, wiping away a few more drops of blood from his mouth, "I will not trouble you for much   longer."
Cries of no, no greeted this obvious plea for sympathy, though not quite so many as he would have liked. Grinning, he looked around the table until he spotted his guest.

Pascent had remained standing when the others sat, and bowed formally when Ambrosius' eyes fell upon him.

"Prince Pascent," said Ambrosius, "you are welcome to court. Where is your noble mother?"

"She sends her apologies, lord," Pascent replied, "a fever confines her to bed, and she was unable to make the journey."

Ambrosius pondered whether this was a lie. But why should Sevira attempt to deceive him? She had never been his enemy.

He thrust aside his doubts. They were not worthy of him, and there was nothing unlikely about Sevira falling ill. She was an old woman now, well past the age most women reached. Best to leave her in peace.

"I shall pray for her swift recovery," he said kindly, "take your seat on the council, and be assured of my trust and friendship."

Pascent bowed again, and sat between Eidol Cadarn and Meurig ap Tewdrig, King of Glamorgan.

Ambrosius had plans for Pascent. A seat on the council wasn't enough. To secure his loyalty, Ambrosius meant to offer him Brecon, a small kingdom immediately to the south-west of his father's territory in Powys.

This would be some compensation for being denied his larger inheritance. The prosperous city of Viroconium and its surrounding lands was to come under the direct control of the council. The Cornovii were far too numerous and powerful to be trusted, and Ambrosius wanted to prevent the rise of another

Vortigern, with hundreds of tribal warriors at his back and designs on the High Kingship.

A slave poured wine into his cup. His hand shook slightly as he raised the cup to his lips and took a long swallow.

The wine was spiced, and blood-warm. Ambrosius was fond of strong hot wine. It helped to quell his sickness, at least for a few hours.

He closed his eyes for a moment, relishing the liquid fire pouring down his throat.

"Let us eat," he said eventually, "and discuss the business of government later."

He relaxed in his chair, resting his back against the hard wood, letting the murmur of conversation and the slow, insistent melody of a harp wash over him. The delicious smell of roasted meat and fresh bread reached his nostrils as slaves moved to and fro with heaped platters of food.

Once, the smell would have pricked his appetite. No longer. Ambrosius ate little these days, and his stomach rebelled at anything stronger than broth.

"The fire is too hot," he muttered, wiping the sweat from his brow, "have the slaves douse it. Winter is not here just yet."

"There is no fire, father," said Artorius, who was busily tearing apart half a roast chicken with his big, powerful hands.

Of course there is no fire, Ambrosius chided himself, *what am I thinking? The palace is warmed by the hypocaust.*

The heat was oppressive. His skin prickled with it. He was reminded of Bishop Germanus, who wore a hair shirt under his robes. Ambrosius felt as though a hair shirt had somehow grown under his flesh.

He reached for the wine jug, but his fingers were clumsy and knocked the elegantly fluted vessel over. Red liquid flowed across the table and dripped over the edge, pooling on the flagstones.

Slaves rushed to clean up the spillage. Ambrosius ignored them. His throat was suddenly bone-dry. Not just dry, but constricting, as though ghostly hands were doing their best to throttle him.

Vortigern's hands.

Gasping and clutching at his neck, he glanced up and saw Pascent staring at him. The prince's mild blue eyes were wide and full of terror.

Not terror. Guilt.

Poison!

The word drove through Ambrosius' mind like a spear. His breath rasped as he struggled to speak, to form words, to throw them at his assassin.

All these years he has nursed a grudge for the death of his father! All these years, and not a word, not a hint of conspiracy from him! He waited for me to invite him here, like a foolish old hen, inviting the fox into the coop.

The rest of the councillors stood up, a sea of concerned voices and frowning faces. Ambrosius' vision dimmed. The pain in his throat and chest were unbearable, like two lengths of steel wire cutting into his flesh.

Through the rushing of blood in his ears, he heard the voices of his friends.

"Give him space!" shouted Cunedda, "he must have air – fetch the apothecary, quickly!"

Too late. No remedy could arrive in time to dilute the poison racing like quicksilver through his veins.

"Father!" Artorius' voice, thick with grief and fear. The young man's powerful arms cradled his head.

It falls to you now, Ambrosius wanted to say, but the power of speech had left him. Artorius' face was just inches from his own, horribly blurred.

The bands tightened. Breath refused to come. Ambrosius' vision faded to black. Even the pain was ebbing.

His last thought was of his daughter. Morgana's pale face, her bandaged eyes, appeared briefly before him. She raised a finger to her lips.

Then nothing.

25.

The funeral procession moved slowly along the highway from Londinium to Mons Ambrius, where Ambrosius was to be laid to rest next to his father.

A suitably magnificent escort had been arranged for his last journey. His body lay inside a stone sarcophagus mounted on a six-wheeled carriage, drawn by twelve horses. The bier was guarded by a company of Ambrosius' buccelari, veterans who had served him in all his battles. More mounted companies rode before it at a slow trot, while a long line of black-robed monks shuffled along behind, chanting dreary psalms.

Artorius rode at the head of the procession under his adoptive father's dragon banner. He considered this his right, since he had arranged the funeral, and was Ambrosius' heir.

Heir to what, though? Strangely, for a man usually so meticulous and organised in his affairs, Ambrosius had never made an official will. He had always put it off, claiming that he intended to live many years yet.

Artorius suspected that he had secretly feared death, and preferred not to think of it. Death had come for him regardless, in the form of a poisoned chalice of wine, and left Britannia without her defender and guide.

People flocked from the towns and villages to watch their departed lord go to his rest. Many of them wept at the sight of the sarcophagus, and cast wondering glances at the tall fair-haired man on the white horse at the head of the procession.

"That is the soldier Artorius," he heard them whisper to each other, "he will protect us now."

The soldier Artorius. Is that all he was? Ambrosius had meant him to assume supreme civilian as well as military authority. There were plenty who might contest his right to anything more than the title he already held, Magister Equitum.

I have the soldiers on my side, he thought, *and several of the councillors are my friends.*

AMBROSIUS

He felt no guilt at contemplating his own future before Ambrosius was even laid in the ground. A man had to look to his own survival. Artorius' thoughts were roughly divided between self-interest, genuine sorrow for Ambrosius, and determination to avenge him.

Ambrosius' killer was yet unknown. Many suspected Pascent, since he had the most obvious motive, but there was no proof. The slave who served the poisoned wine had been thoroughly interrogated, but clearly knew nothing. The hand that slipped the poison into the wine was a subtle one.

Pascent, along with the other councillors, was due to attend the funeral at Mons Ambrius. Even now their retinues would be converging on the fortress. Those closest to Artorius – Cei, Bedwyr and Gwalchmei - had chosen to accompany him from the capital.

Artorius suspected Pascent would stay away. If so, it would be a clear admission of guilt, and his life was forfeit. Artorius would relish hunting him down and spilling the last of the accursed blood of Vortigern.

The procession slowly made its way over the rolling downs and hill country of the west, descending to the fertile plains near Mons Ambrius. On the way it passed the dreaded henge, the stone circle where Hengist's Saxons had treacherously slaughtered the Council of Britannia. Their blood had watered the earth, just like the blood of the hapless victims once sacrificed there by the druids of antiquity.

It was dusk, and the ancient monoliths loomed larger than ever in the half-light of the dying sun, casting monstrous shadows across the ground. Artorius shuddered, and made the sign of the cross. This was an evil place.

A hooded and cloaked figure stepped out of the shadows of the outer circle and halted by the roadside. Two thin white hands pushed back the hood to reveal a female face, pale as death, her eyes covered by a silken bandage.

The woman flung up her arms as the first of the riders neared, and spoke in surprisingly deep, ringing tones that carried across the plain.

219

"Oh irreparable loss! Oh bereaved people of Britannia! Gone is the illustrious soldier, the shield of your race! The renowned champion of the Britons, Ambrosius Aurelianus, is dead! His death will prove fatal to us all, unless God be our helper. Make haste, therefore, most noble Artorius, make haste to engage the enemy. The victory will be yours, and you shall rule all Britannia. The soul of Ambrosius ascends to the heavens, and you are the fiery dragon he leaves to defend his earthly realm."

"Be silent, witch," growled Cei, "crawl off back to your hole, else I put the flat of my sword to you."

"Peace, Cei," said Artorius, "I think this is no witch, but Ambrosius' daughter Morgana. Am I right, my lady?"

He had never met Morgana, but knew she was blind, and wore a cloth over her useless eyes. There was something of Ambrosius in her slender build, pale features and curling black hair.

"I am the one who was given sight beyond sight," she replied calmly, undeterred by Cei's threat, "my old name no longer carries any meaning. God commanded me to forsake the convent and wander the land in search of His lost secrets. I have been reborn as the Seer of Britannia."

Cei snorted. "Her father's death has driven her mad," he said mockingly, "leave her be, else she puts a spell on us."

Artorius ignored him. "Sister," he said gently, "why do you give us this warning? I know my duty."

Morgana remained silent. Artorius sensed that she was somehow reading him, raking over his soul with a perception he could not begin to understand.

"Follow me to the stones," she said at last, turning her back on him. Despite her apparent blindness, she strode confidently back towards the henge with no hesitation in her step.

"Ignore her," said Bedwyr, "Cei is right. The poor woman has run mad."

Artorius thought for a moment, and then slid from the saddle. "Carry on to Mons Ambrius," he ordered, "I will follow later."

They protested, but should have known better: once he had made a decision, nothing could deflect Artorius from his chosen path. While the bier and its escort continued on to the hill-fort, he led his horse towards the stones.

Artorius tethered the beast to one of the larger of the bits of rubble strewn about the outer circle, and walked on alone to the inner.

Morgana was waiting for him beside the altar-stone. He shivered at the sight of the huge fallen slab. It was a warm evening, but a strange chill permeated the stones. This was a place of death, of blood and treachery and ancient cruelties.

His eye fell on a sword laid on the slab. Morgana's left hand rested on the hilt, and the blade was hidden inside a wooden sheath.

"Brother," she said, facing him, "come and take your sword."

Artorius stood between two of the mighty uprights, capped with a lintel. He was reluctant to enter the circle.

"I already have one," he replied, patting the spatha hanging from his hip, "and that thing you hold is no use to me. It's a Roman gladius. An old infantry weapon, made for stabbing in the melee. I have no need of it."

"You have need of this."

She pulled the sword free of its sheath and held the blade upright before her face. A beam of light from the setting sun rippled down its length. Artorius noticed the hilt was made of ivory, and stamped with two golden eagles.

"Caesar's sword," she intoned, "known to the Romans as The Red Death. Forged on Mount Olympus by Vulcan, the smith-god. Wielded by Julius Caesar himself when he came to these shores and engaged in single combat with Nennius, Prince of the Trinovantes."

She advanced towards him, holding the gladius towards him, hilt-first. "Before he died of his wounds, Nennius named the sword Caledfwlch, and laid a curse on it. Only a true King of Britannia can wield the sword. For over four hundred years it has lain hidden in the earth beside Nennius' body, waiting. Waiting for you."

Artorius backed away. He knew the old story of Caesar and Nennius, but regarded it as a myth, fit only for children.

221

"I am no king," he said, "the sword you carry is a fake. No-one knows where Nennius was buried, or if he ever really lived."

Morgana smiled. "You forget what I am, brother. What God has tasked me to do. I seek out lost secrets. Take the sword. With Caledfwlch at your side, you can unite the people of Britannia. None will dare challenge your authority."

Artorius froze. Something about Morgana, her voice, the strange power radiating from her, frightened him. She moved closer, and Caledfwlch rose before him, filling his vision, his world.

"Take it."

She spoke with terrible, undeniable conviction. Ambition and fear warred inside his breast.

He reached out, and his fingers closed around the hilt.

AUTHOR'S NOTE

I avoided writing this book for a long time. There are so many novels by so many great writers dealing with the 'history' behind Arthurian legend out there, it seemed futile, not to say a little presumptuous, to toss my own effort onto the pile.

Recently it struck me that the age-old story could be approached from a (relatively) fresh angle by concentrating first on Ambrosius Aurelianus, an obscure figure, largely hidden behind the gigantic shadow of Arthur. Unlike Arthur, however, we can be reasonably certain that Ambrosius existed, and led the Romano-British resistance against the Saxons.

The Dark Ages are suitably named. A blank curtain lies over British history from c.400-600 AD, between the departure of the Roman legions and the rise of the Saxon kingdoms. Modern archaeology is helping us to discover more about the period, but the sheer lack of written sources remains a crippling problem in trying to piece together events.

One of the very few surviving sources is *De Excidio de Conquestu Britanniae,* or 'On the Ruin and Conquest of Britannia', written by a somewhat mysterious and irritating British cleric named Gildas. Probably written in the first quarter of the sixth century, it is intended as a sermon in three parts rather than a history. Gildas doesn't mince his words, and uses the history of Britannia from the coming of the Romans as a stick to beat the British rulers of his own day, lambasting them as lazy, sinful and incompetent.

In fact, Gildas doesn't have a good word to say about almost anyone. One of the few to escape his censure is Ambrosius, who he describes as 'the last of the Romans' and the man who ignited the British resistance against the marauding Saxons in the mid-5th century, about a hundred years before the time of writing.

Gildas says Ambrosius was 'a modest man' whose parents 'wore the purple', probably implying they were of consular or senatorial rank. Following the initial shock of the Saxon revolt, the Britons fled to Ambrosius 'as eagerly as bees to a beehive when a storm threatens'. Under his leadership, they regained their strength, and challenged the Saxons to battle. The war raged on for an uncertain length of time – Gildas is frustratingly vague on dates – with victories and defeats on either side, until the year of the 'siege of Mons Badonicus', where the Britons finally scored a major victory.

Mons Badonicus, or Mount Badon, is traditionally the career-defining victory won by Arthur, perhaps Britannia's most famous legendary hero. Strangely (or tellingly?) Gildas makes no mention of him. The only British hero he names in connection with the fight against the Saxons is Ambrosius, but he stops short of also naming him the victor of Badon. The earliest feasible dating for Badon is c.482, which makes it a little late for Ambrosius, since the Saxon revolt started some thirty years earlier.

There are ways of reconciling these issues. I prefer to believe that Arthur did exist, and possibly learned his trade as a soldier under Ambrosius, eventually taking over command of the British forces when the latter died or retired. This idea forms the central theme of the *Leader of Battles* series, which will follow the careers of both Ambrosius and Arthur (or Artuír/Artorius as I call him) in their fight to defend Britannia against 'innumerable hordes of foul barbarians', as Churchill put it.

Perhaps understandably, Arthurian novelists have generally been keen to skim over Ambrosius in order to get to the main event, or even omit him altogether. This seems terribly unfair on one of the few definite historical personages we know anything about from this period, and one who initiated the fight-back against his country's enemies.

I wanted to do Ambrosius justice, and make some effort to depict his life and heroic struggle in the dark, shadowy world of post-Roman Britannia, a land of crumbling towns and infrastructure, living under constant fear of barbarian invasion. The final, desperate appeal made by the Britons to the Roman military sums up the general mood of chaos and despair:

"To Agitius, thrice Consul: the groans of the Britons. The barbarians drive us to the sea, the sea drives us to the barbarians;

between these two means of death, we are either killed or drowned…"

The Romans, however, had their own problems to deal with, and Britannia was left to fend for itself. For a time, the dwindling light of Roman civilisation was kept alive by a succession of British military leaders. Ambrosius Aurelianus was the first of them, and the tale of his more famous successor will be told in Book Two.

One final note: the *Leader of Battles* series can be read as loose prequels to my *Caesar's Sword* trilogy, which describes the adventures of Coel ap Ahmar, Arthur's grandson, in the glittering but deadly world of Constantinople and the Eastern Empire.

Printed in Great Britain
by Amazon

25136571R00131